Neoliberal Bodies and the Fat Body

In recent decades the rise of the so-called "global obesity epidemic" has led to fatness and fat bodies being debated incessantly in popular, professional, and academic arenas. Fatness and fat bodies are shamed and demonised, and the public monitoring, surveillance and outright policing by the media, health professionals, and the general public are pervasive and socially accepted.

In *Neoliberal Bodies and the Gendered Fat Body*, Hannele Harjunen claims that neoliberal economic policy and rationale are enmeshed with conceptions of body, gender, and health in a profound way in contemporary Western culture. She explores the relationships between fatness, health, and neoliberal discourse and the role of economic policy in the construction of the (gendered) fat body, and examines how neoliberal discourses join patriarchal and biomedical constructions of the fat female body. In neoliberal culture the fat body is not just the unhealthy body one finds in medical discourse, but also the body that is costly, unproductive and inefficient, failing in the crucial task of self-management.

With an emphasis on how neoliberal governmentality, in its many forms, affects the fat body and contributes to its vilification, this book is essential reading for scholars of feminist thought, sociology, cultural studies and social theory with interests in the body, gender and the effects of neoliberal discourse on social attitudes.

Hannele Harjunen is Senior Lecturer in Gender Studies in the Department of Social Sciences and Philosophy at the University of Jyväskylä, Finland.

Routledge Research in Gender and Society

Neoliberal Bodies and the Gendered Fat Body

Hannele Harjunen

LONDON AND NEW YORK

First published 2017 by Routledge

2 Park Square, Milton Park, Abingdon, Oxfordshire OX14 4RN

52 Vanderbilt Avenue, New York, NY 10017

Routledge is an imprint of the Taylor & Francis Group, an informa business

First issued in paperback 2020

British Library Cataloguing in Publication Data
A catalogue record for this book is available from the British Library

Library of Congress Cataloging in Publication Data
Names: Harjunen, Hannele, author.
Title: Neoliberal bodies and the gendered fat body / Hannele S. Harjunen.
Description: Abingdon, Oxon ; New York, NY : Routledge, 2016. |
    Series: Routledge research in gender and society ; 52 | Includes
    bibliographical references and index.
Identifiers: LCCN 2016005148| ISBN 9781472431400 (hardback) |
    ISBN 9781315583976 (ebook)
Subjects: LCSH: Human body—Social aspects. | Neoliberalism—Social
    aspects. | Obesity—Social aspects. | Obesity in women—Social
    aspects. | Public health. | Feminist theory.
Classification: LCC HM636 .H355 2016 | DDC 305.4201—dc23
LC record available at http://lccn.loc.gov/2016005148

ISBN: 978-1-4724-3140-0 (hbk)
ISBN: 978-0-367-59621-7 (pbk)

Typeset in Times New Roman
by Swales & Willis Ltd, Exeter, Devon, UK

Contents

Acknowledgements

This book would not be possible without the support and encouragement of many individuals and institutions. I am especially grateful to my colleagues at the University of Jyväskylä for their constant support and daily intellectual sustenance. Discussions with my closest colleagues at the Department of Social Sciences and Philosophy – Helena Hirvonen, Laura Mankki, Mikko Jakonen, and Miira Tuominen, in particular – have helped me a great deal along the way. Matti Roitto and Melissa Plath helped me with the manuscript when I most needed it. Many others have generously commented on chapters of this book during seminars and conferences.

Especially, I want to thank my long-time colleague and writing partner Katariina Kyrölä for her invaluable feedback and guidance at different stages of this project. I also need to thank the amazing community of fat studies scholars that I have had a chance to meet at the Popular Culture Association conference in the United States annually since 2009. Many of the chapters included in this book, I have presented first to this inspiring and supportive group of colleagues. Over the years both their feedback and academic companionship have proven invaluable.

As always, I am grateful to the University of Jyväskylä for their continual support of my work. In particular, I am thankful for the travel grant that gave me a chance to concentrate on writing this book away from my daily routines for two months at a critical stage of the writing process. I also need to express my gratitude to my colleague and writing partner Jeannine Gailey for inspiration, collegiality, and all the good times in Fort Worth, Texas. She and the wonderful people at the Department of Sociology and Anthropology at TCU made me feel welcome in every possible way.

I am fortunate enough to have an amazing tightknit group of friends, many of whom are also colleagues. Some of the most important advice regarding this work and life in general has come from this group of people over drinks in our local. Thank you, Johanna Kivimäki, Lasse Immonen, Onni Pekonen, Laura Piippo, Vesa Plath, Pedro Rodriguez, and Antti Vesikko.

1 Introduction and personal prologue

This book is the result of a long personal and professional interest in questions concerning gender, body norms, and the social construction of what is considered a "normal" (female) body. In particular, the body which exceeds the body size norm, and is variously named as the fat, overweight, or obese body depending on the discourse and context, has been a constant focus in my work.

Like many other researchers, my own experience and background first led me to this topic. Before I began to study fatness[1] academically, I already had some experience of the phenomenon from living in a fat body. I grew up as a fat kid, lost weight in my early teens, was a normative-sized teenager for a few years, struggled to keep the weight off for years, lost and gained weight by turns after this, and by the time I was a twenty-something university student, I was fat again. It could be said that because of my own experience of living in a body that was considered non-normative, i.e., fat, and also in a body that was normative-sized, I have had access to experiential knowledge of the social effects of body size. For example, in school, which is one of the key sites of learning about body norms and hierarchy (e.g. Harjunen 2002; Kosonen 1998), I learnt at an early age that not only does one's body size influence how people treat you, but that the experience of fatness is also gendered. In other words, it is considered especially undesirable to be a fat girl or woman. Lesko (1988), for example, has referred to this gendered learning about the body in school as the "curriculum of the body". I also knew – from trying, succeeding, and failing – what research on dieting has confirmed over the years: namely that after losing weight, maintaining weight loss is a difficult feat to accomplish in the long run (e.g. Sarlio-Lähteenkorva 1999).

In addition to this self-observed knowledge of the effects of fatness in social relations and the social environment, I also gained first-hand experience on how one's body size becomes a site of medical intervention and a target of institutional efforts to control it already as a young child. The first time I was put on a diet suggested by a medical professional was when I was seven years old. After a medical check-up by a school nurse, I was deemed too heavy for my age according to the height/weight charts, and an appointment with a paediatrician and a dietician at the local hospital was booked. I do not remember much about the discussions that took place during that appointment, but I do remember that I was given a sheet of paper that contained a list of foods that I was not supposed to eat and what was recommended instead. I recall that there were some curious items and brand names on the list of recommended products such as diet soda called "Slim" and sugar-free biscuits that were meant for people with diabetes. As I did not yet understand what dieting was, or that you needed special products for it, the list was neither very useful to me, nor was I in control of my own diet.

Although I cannot recall any significant changes to my diet, I do remember that after that hospital appointment, my mother started to comment on my eating and tried to control the size of my portions during meals, which frequently led to tension and arguments between us. I did not lose weight then, as far as I can remember, so in that sense this was not exactly a successful intervention. However, this episode was significant, in that it was my initiation into the world of dieting, commercial diet culture, and weight monitoring as an integral part of life. At the age of seven I started to learn that my body was a problem, it was not the way it was supposed to be, and that it was my responsibility to do something about it. In retrospect, it is worth noting that I did not learn about the normality of thinness and undesirability of fatness from the media, nor from being exposed to unattainable feminine beauty and body norms and ideals from an early age – these are often named as the main culprits and the primary source of female body image issues – yet the message was clear.

Indeed, governing the body and learning about body norms takes place in everyday settings and everyday life (e.g. Harjunen 2002; Haug 1987).

I did not comprehend it at the time, but what essentially happened was that my body weight and size had not only become an issue of "biopower" and "biopolitical concern" (see Foucault 1990), but also a site for disciplinary action and punishment. My body was now under surveillance, my weight was monitored, and I learnt the art of self-regulation and self-governing. It could be said that I have lived inside of a biopolitical "weight panopticon" for most of my life (see e.g. Foucault 1979, pp. 200–201). Another way that I have learnt to see this is in terms of the notion of "biopedagogy" used in Wright and Harwood (2011) to refer to those normalising and disciplining practices that have been created to assess, monitor, and discipline fat bodies, or bodies that are considered at risk of becoming fat. The school environment is one typical site for biopedagogies, although obviously not the only one.

I learnt more about the importance of controlling the body weight and body size when my weight became an issue again a few years later. One day at school, every child had to go for a check-up at the school's health centre. When my turn came to see the doctor, I was weighed and I remember actually being scolded by the doctor about my weight. During the visit to the paediatrician years earlier, my mother was with me and she was given advice on proper nutrition and exercise. This time I was on my own in the doctor's office. I was not given any advice on what to do or how to go on a diet, nor offered any type of support or supervision. I was simply told that I was too fat and needed to lose weight. I was very upset after seeing the doctor and I can remember the feeling of shame and rejection. It was primarily the doctor's words that prompted me to go on a diet for the first time on my own soon after. His "curing by shaming" method was in this sense effective, albeit unethical and abusive. On my wall at home, I put up a poster that displayed the calorific content of different foodstuffs, that I had found in some women's magazine, and started meticulously counting calories. I then went on to lose a significant amount of weight through a self-made diet that in hindsight was very restrictive and nutritionally inadequate for a growing pre-teen.

It seems evident that, considering current knowledge on the aetiology of eating disorders (and the prevalence and severity of various body image problems), the comments of the school doctor were particularly ill-advised. It has been well established that, for example, body-shaming comments can trigger eating disorders and encourage the development of dangerous dieting habits (e.g. Noll and Fredrickson 1998). But in all fairness, the doctor was not the only one who was thoughtless in his choice of words; awareness of body image issues was generally lower at that time. Nowadays, it would be considered worrying if a twelve-year-old girl went on a diet and lost about fifteen kilograms during one school year without any supervision. In hindsight, there was potentially a high risk for developing an eating disorder then and there. However, in the mid-1980s, no one expressed any concern over it, as far as I can remember. On the contrary, everybody (from friends and their parents to teachers) thought that it was great I was getting slimmer, and I received only encouragement and praise for my weight loss. In essence, I was shamed into dieting by an adult in a position of medical authority and then left to solve the problem in the only way that I could see was available to me – by going on a diet. Furthermore, I was socially rewarded for losing weight, even though it had happened in an unsupervised and probably unhealthy way. My experience is an all-too-common example of what happens when the mechanically applied medical paradigm of "fatness as health hazard" is combined with a narrow conception of the normal body, an emphasis on individual responsibility, and the social stigma of being fat. Unfortunately, research informs us that this is also generally representative of fat people's experiences regarding their treatment by medical/health professionals (e.g. Brownell and Teachman 2000; Harjunen 2009; Puhl and Brownell 2001).

When, as a graduate student, I started thinking about studying fatness in academic terms, I had already learnt from my own personal experience that fatness was both a medical and social issue. Furthermore, it was clear that fatness was a gendered experience with particular significance for women. However, this experiential knowledge of fatness as being something socially significant was not yet reflected in the academic literature in the mid-1990s. I first became interested in academic research of fatness then as an undergraduate student whilst writing a paper for a women's studies class on ideals of beauty and the body. While looking for existing research I soon became aware of the medical bias that existed, and how poorly fatness was understood as a social and sociological issue. At the time, there was no domestic (Finnish) and very little international non-medical research on fatness, on fat female bodies (or male for that matter), or the experience of being fat. I was quite surprised to discover that these subjects, never mind the experiences of fat people, were so under-theorised and under-researched. Most surprising of all was the seeming lack of interest in feminist academic circles in addressing the topic of fatness and the fat body, although there was already a mass of feminist critique dealing with oppressive body norms and the thin ideal (e.g. Bartky 1990; Bordo 1993; Orbach 1998 [1977 and 1982]; Wolf 1991). The fat body was in a way "present but absent" – always there in the background, but clearly not the focal point of feminist study on gendered body norms. Although I knew that there were feminist fat activists and a fat acceptance movement in the US and the UK, I had no access to them as an academic resource, and there was no organised fat activist movement in Finland. My academic work on fatness was thus initially motivated by the absence of the fat body and fat experience in both feminist studies and social research in general.

Since the mid-1990s a great deal has happened: fatness has become a global issue that is continually talked about in any number of forums. It is certainly not an invisible issue any longer. My active years as a researcher have, in fact, coincided with the rise of the so-called "global obesity epidemic" and accompanying "obesity epidemic discourse" (e.g. LeBesco 2010; Murray 2008, p. 15). Since the turn of the century, fatness and fat bodies have been debated incessantly in popular, professional, and academic arenas. In the media, fatness has been a topic of countless newspaper headlines, feature articles, internet forum discussions, documentaries, talk shows, and diet and makeover programmes. In the field of public health policy and health promotion, fatness has been the focus of numerous prevention and action programmes, conferences, awareness and weight loss campaigns, and the target of policies that are purely disciplinary in nature. In addition to these popular and health policy discourses, during the past decade or so there has been a notable upsurge of interest in the study of fatness in academia (see Saguy and Riley 2005). This "obesity epidemic rhetoric" has given a push, paradoxically, to both "obesity science" based on biomedicine (Gard and Wright 2005; Rail, Holmes, and Murray, 2010) and interdisciplinary critical and feminist fat studies that denounces it together with the medicalisation of fatness in general (see e.g. Rothblum and Solovay 2009). There is also a great deal of work that is somewhere between these two poles of research activity around fatness.

Today, the discussion on fatness seems positively omnipresent, and in most cases it is still seen through the lens of biomedicine. Fatness is approached firstly as a biomedical issue: it is considered as a problem, threat, and danger to the public and the individual's health. This problem-centred approach to fatness has been promoted especially by proponents of the so-called "obesity epidemic discourse" (OED) that has dominated reporting, research, and debate on fatness since the early 2000s. The obesity epidemic discourse rests on the assumption that fatness is a disease-like condition that is spreading through the world at an uncontrollable pace and in epidemic proportions (e.g. Boero 2012; Gard and Wright 2005; Oliver 2006).

Concern over public health is certainly at the heart of this globally declared "war against obesity" (e.g. Biltekoff 2007; Herndon 2005; Kyrölä 2007). However, not only has it had the effect of stepping up the search for solutions and/or policies to make people fitter and healthier; it has also led to the demonisation of fatness and fat people. Talk of an obesity epidemic intensified the moralising manner in which fat bodies and fat people were already being discussed. Among other things, fat people have been blamed for destroying public healthcare systems and the public economy; fat bodies are continually shamed and ridiculed in public; and fatness has been used as a sign of individual and general moral decay in society (e.g. Farrell 2011; Kyrölä 2014; LeBesco 2011). The obesity epidemic discourse and the moral panic that has ensued have undoubtedly contributed to further stigmatisation of fatness and fat people.[2] For instance, Farrell (2011) and LeBesco (2010) have aptly referred to this combination of moral panic mixed with talk of an obesity epidemic as the "fat panic" (Farrell 2011; LeBesco 2010).

This "fat panic" has proved particularly harmful, as it has enforced the fat stigma by linking the fat body to an individual moral failing – widely seen as a choice and the individual's own failure to control their body. The assumed "choice" to be fat (out of moral incompetence) is then used to justify the discrimination and shaming of fat people. The obesity epidemic discourse has made the stigmatisation of fatness more widespread, public, and socially acceptable. Public monitoring, surveillance and outright "policing" of (fat) bodies by the media, health professionals, and even the general public is pervasive. It has helped to construct fatness as one of the most talked about medical, social, political and moral issues worldwide and made fatness a personal characteristic that is very stigmatising (e.g. Boero 2012; Herndon 2005; Saguy 2013; Skeggs 2005).

I have previously written about the social construction of fatness, fatness as a social issue, and Finnish women's experiences of being fat. I have drawn particularly from feminist research and Foucauldian thought on the body, biopolitics and biopower and focused on the "powers" that construct the fat body[3] (in this case the medicalisation, stigmatisation, and liminalisation[4] of fatness), and biopolitical efforts to normalise the fat female body. The biopolitical control of fatness may certainly have been on the public health promotion agenda before there was any talk of an obesity epidemic, but the discourse clearly turned the issue into a new kind of all-round problem in the public consciousness (Harjunen 2009).

The obesity epidemic discourse constructs obesity as a health risk and a disease, but it has also forcibly promoted it as a social problem (LeBesco 2011), a moral threat (Gard and Wright 2005), and most of all as an economic issue (Ayo 2012; Guthman and DuPuis 2006; Harrison 2012). It seems that the obesity epidemic discourse really took off after the year 2000; and the reasons given for the need to "manage" or "govern" fatness have since then become increasingly economic. At the centre of the obesity epidemic discourse is the assumed economic cost of fatness and the stereotype that fat people are morally corrupt, lazy gluttons, and that the fat body is the result of excessive over-consuming. The relationship between the economy and fatness, however, is not this straightforward or one-dimensional. Today, it seems that economic rationale organises the matter of fatness in a more profound way. A complex meta-level discussion in which fatness and the economy have become closely intertwined with each other can thus be identified.

This book is called *Neoliberal Bodies and the Gendered Fat Body*; and as its title suggests, fatness, gender, and neoliberal thought are at the centre of my investigation. I claim that neoliberal economic policy and rationale are enmeshed with conceptions of body, gender, and health in a profound way in contemporary Western culture. I am particularly interested in the relationships between fatness, health, and neoliberal discourse and the role of economic policy in the construction of the (gendered) fat body. Against the backdrop of the dominant political economic rationale of neoliberalism (Harvey 2007), the fat body has been ranked as an "expensive" body, but not just that; it is almost as if the fat body is constructed as a kind of "anti-neoliberal" body that is unproductive, ineffective, and unprofitable. Furthermore, in the neoliberal imagination, fatness, gender, and socioeconomic class seem to be bound together materially, symbolically, and morally.

The "war against fatness" (see e.g. Biltekoff 2007) that the obesity epidemic discourse partly sparked off, can be seen as a part of a larger social trend that has been shaping up in the Western world since the late 1960s, which links such phenomena as rising health consciousness and healthism, neoliberal economic policy and "the ideology of individual responsibility" (Crawford 1980; 2006). The obesity epidemic discourse can perhaps be seen as the culmination of certain material and discursive developments in society that have occurred over the past forty years. Links between it and neoliberalism have been observed in previous studies to some extent (e.g. Ayo 2012; Guthman and DuPuis 2006; Harrison 2012; LeBesco 2011), but less attention has been dedicated, so far, to analysis that locates gender and the gendered body in these contexts (see Guthman 2009; Heywood 2007). The need for such analysis is highly topical however, as the obesity epidemic discourse, healthism, and neoliberalism are each gendering and gendered discourses of power. In today's parlance, health is often equated with beauty and attempts to create a normative-looking body, especially in the context of commercialised and neoliberally charged health. Women, and women's bodies in particular, are targeted and governed through the healthist, fat-phobic, and commercialised health discourse (e.g. Dworkin and Wachs 2009; Heywood 2007; Markula 2008).

One purpose of this book is to expand on this discussion and explore these relationships further. It has been well established that two major discourses, patriarchal and biomedical, have been especially influential in determining the boundaries of the normative female body. Patriarchal notions of the role and status of women in society as the "second sex" (see de Beauvoir, 1949), combined with a biomedical understanding of the normal and healthy (female) body, in particular, have shaped and continue to shape what kind of (female) bodies are valued, considered desirable, or just plain acceptable in society. These discourses have also helped define what is considered appropriate behaviour for women, and how women should use their bodies. Patriarchal and biomedical discourses concerning the female body are embodied and they are played out in everyday life.

In this book though, I want to bring forward a third major discourse that should join the patriarchal and biomedical; if we wish to study today's social construction of the female body (in terms of its size), or indeed, if we are to look at body politics in general, I believe we must include neoliberalism. Neoliberalism is an all-pervading discourse and global economic policy that shapes the manner we approach, see, and evaluate gendered bodies, and how we live in them. In fact, neoliberal rationale seems to add a new layer of normative expectations on top of the existing ones that determine the boundaries of normal and/or feminine bodies. The gendered embodied people of today have to negotiate their position between patriarchal, biomedical, and neoliberal capitalist expectations. Although these three discourses can be identified and examined separately, they are also mutually constitutive and overlapping in many contexts – such as, for example, discussions concerning gender and the body, health or fitness, and commercial culture (e.g. Dworkin and Wachs 2009; Heywood 2011; Markula 2008).

Next I will briefly explore the premise, key themes, and concepts of this book in greater detail; starting with neoliberalism, then going on to the body, fatness, and the obesity epidemic. I will start with a short discussion on neoliberalism and what I mean when using the concepts "neoliberal culture" and "neoliberal body" in this work, and how they are connected to fatness and the fat body. In addition, the methodology and data used in this book will be presented, and I will end the chapter by drawing an outline of the other chapters in the book.

Neoliberal society, neoliberal bodies?

The foremost economic approach in the Western world since the 1980s has been that of neoliberalism (Harvey 2007). During the past thirty years, neoliberal economic policy and rationale have shaped the world we live in. Neoliberalism is a distinctly market-driven approach and over the past decades its logic, discourse and practice have been promoted actively and adopted locally and globally. It has been argued that neoliberal rationale has permeated political and social discourses and its effects are now visible at practically all levels of society. Key elements of neoliberal economic policy, such as minimal public intervention and deregulation of the market, privatisation of the public domain, an emphasis on cost-effectiveness, productivity, and profit have become an integral part of all aspects of public as well as private life (e.g. Brown 2003; Harvey 2007; Ventura 2012).

Social structures and institutions have been transformed by neoliberal policies that put the interests of the market first. For instance, in Finland and other Nordic countries, significant institutional changes and restructuring have taken place due to a change in political ethos that prioritises economic efficiency above all else (e.g. Dahlgren 2008; Eräsaari 2002). Neoliberal policies have been gradually replacing, have already replaced, or have at least reduced the scope of welfare state policies. The principles of universalism and egalitarianism, which provided the basis of the welfare state, have been replaced by the neoliberal principles of effectiveness and productivity (Wrede *et al.* 2008, p. 17). This has meant, among other things, a decrease and outsourcing of services, cuts to social benefits and in general, a more business-oriented organisation of the public sector in the form of so-called "new public management", or NPM for short (Yliaska 2014).

The adoption of a neoliberal rationale affects not only public structures and institutions, however. People's private lives have been transformed too. A neoliberal way of thinking has entered even the most intimate parts of life such as eating, exercising, and taking care of the body. It could be suggested that neoliberalism as a form of governmentality (see e.g. Brown 2003; Lemke 2001; Oksala 2013) has come to inform and steer our understanding of bodies, how we live in them, and the relationship we are supposed to enjoy with them. This neoliberal governmentality regarding the body is evident, for instance, in the various ways gendered bodies are commodified and commercialised (Gill 2007; 2008), or how health has become increasingly about personal responsibility (Crawford 2006) and consumption (Conrad 2007).

Above all, the ideal neoliberal subject is a master of self-governing (Gill 2007; 2008). That is, they are pictured as free and independent, responsible and rational, and continually striving to be in control of their bodies and physical actions. Interestingly, stressing the freedom and choice of individuals does not seem to make people "freer", at least in relation to their bodies. In fact, paradoxically enough, the neoliberal approach to the body is not "liberal" at all, as it seems to produce a great deal of stress and worry. One must put in tremendous effort and work to be able to present a controlled "neoliberal body" that expresses neoliberal values. One's body is taken as a sign of the effort put into it. Indeed, hours put into "body work" have become a part of the new requirement for individual productivity.

The embodied neoliberal subject appears to be imbued with conflicting demands and expectations: individuals are seemingly offered the freedom to choose to do what they want with their bodies, and moreover, bestowed with a moral and social responsibility to do so. Yet power over determining the options from which to choose, and how to be responsible for this, lie elsewhere. Indeed, it has been argued that neoliberalism creates individuals who, through contradictory impulses of free choice and responsibility, become "hyper-vigilant of control and self-discipline" (Guthman 2009, p. 193), or as Wendy Brown succinctly puts it: people have become "controlled through their freedom" (2003, p. 7).

With all the emphasis on such principles as control, discipline, productivity, and cost-effectiveness that extend from structures to individuals, it does not seem entirely by chance that fatness and fat bodies have become especially feared and reviled in the neoliberal era. Fatness had certainly been regarded as an undesirable and stigmatised characteristic before; fatness and the fat body have been associated with negative social and moral traits for a long time (e.g. Farrell 2011; Huff 2001). The fat body has been commonly perceived as the unruly and excessive body (Braziel Evans and LeBesco 2001; LeBesco 2004), and a body that is in desperate need of measuring, medicating, and normalising; in other words, it needs biopolitical governing (Harjunen 2009). However, the extent to which fat phobia now exists in society is quite unprecedented.

Rodan, Ellis, and Lebeck (2014, p. 8), who have studied representations of fatness in popular media, say that fatness – alongside other characteristics such as disability and ageing – has begun to represent a lack of control of the body.

They further argue that such characteristics represent "states of being" that are uncomfortable to those who want to believe that they are in control of their bodies, an assertion which the neoliberal ethos encourages us all to internalise. The fat body's visual appearance as a body that is "out of bounds" (see Braziel Evans and LeBesco 2001) and stereotypical qualities that are associated with such a body, like self-indulgence, greediness, laziness, and lack of self-restraint, thus also suggest a subject that is out of control. Fat bodies breach the ideal of a controlled embodied subject both materially and discursively, and are a constant reminder of the body's potential uncontrollability, i.e., the uncontrollability of life itself.

The moral panic that the obesity epidemic discourse has created around fatness in the contemporary Western cultural sphere (e.g. Gard and Wright 2005; Harjunen 2004b; LeBesco 2010) seems to suggest that the fat body has become emblematic of failure in the embodied performance of control. This is a grave matter in a culture where the ability to control one's body, most acutely manifested in the ability to control one's body size, has become an all-important standard, not only for health but also attractiveness, social acceptability, morality, and productiveness. In this context, the body's size is taken as a sign of (ir)responsibility in a larger context than an individual's personal life; it becomes a sign of whether or not one is a proper, deserving, and productive (neoliberal) citizen.

The fat body in neoliberal culture

In this book, I set out to explore the construction of the fat (female) body by patriarchal, biomedical, and neoliberal discourses. Is there a body that could be called a "neoliberal body", and if so, what are its constituents and how might they be interconnected? How are the norms, ideals, and practices concerning the body, fatness, and gender forged in this "neoliberal culture", or at least with its help (to fit its purpose in governing, and gender regime, etc.)? How do we become neoliberal subjects and neoliberal bodies?

My objective here is twofold. First, I intend to look at the ways in which the fat body becomes (and is made) intelligible in the broader context of neoliberal culture. To do this, I will look at where neoliberalism as an economic policy (and form of governmentality) intersects with phenomena that I have identified as occupying key roles in the social construction of fatness – such as medicalisation, healthism, economisation of health, and commodification of the body. Second, I am interested in the way neoliberalism contributes to moulding "acceptable" and "unacceptable", healthy and unhealthy gendered bodies and subjects. My intention is to develop the idea that the emergence of "obesity" as a global phenomenon in the late 1990s and early 2000s is connected to the prevailing "neoliberal culture" and construction of the "neoliberal body".

I have borrowed the notion of "neoliberal culture" from Patricia Ventura (2012). As a concept it not only refers to the economic school of neoliberalism, but also more broadly to organising social realities according to a neoliberal economic rationale.

She argues that the values and norms we follow are very much shaped by a neoliberal logic. Consequently our everyday lives, as well as our bodies, become organised and regulated according to its needs, values, and priorities. In her work, Ventura uses the concept of "neoliberal culture" to describe both the pervasiveness and persuasiveness of neoliberal thought. She argues that it has extended its scope from the realm of economy and now become a part and parcel of American people's everyday life, organisation of the world, and even their "structure of feeling". According to Ventura (2012, p. 2), neoliberalism is at one and the same time an ideology, an economic approach, and a way of thinking. It can be seen as a series, or continuum, of adjoined characteristics. The inclusiveness of Ventura's approach to neoliberal culture is enticing, as it gives room to discuss the complex social phenomena that would otherwise be difficult to explain or grasp by solely concentrating on neoliberalism as just an economic policy. The concept of "neoliberal culture" entails certain elements that together create a dynamic and evolving "mechanism" that incorporates and drives human activity and experience.

Fatness is one such complex and multifaceted issue. My point of departure is that different elements of neoliberal culture find something to latch onto and exploit in the concept of the fat body. Social institutions such as healthcare policies; or structures, such as healthcare systems; not to mention social, moral, and political orders of the day all contribute to conceptually (as well as physically) shaping fat bodies. Indeed, these aspects of neoliberal culture are made more visible via the "obese body" (the biomedical construction of the diseased fat body). According to the rationale of neoliberal culture, the "obese" body has begun to represent the opposite of everything that is held valuable and worth pursuing; and yet all the while the fat body is constructed as the "other", it curiously dominates neoliberal body culture from the side-lines. Could it thus be that the fat body is in fact *the* neoliberal body?

Healthy, acceptable, and moral bodies . . . and their opposites

My second objective relates to the construction of acceptable and unacceptable bodies via conceptions of health. Health, or at least being concerned about it, is a central requirement for all morally and socially responsible individuals today and a normative expectation of them in the age of healthism. The fat body is seen as a sign of ill-health and an illness whether or not it actually is. The biomedical understanding of fatness as an illness, and the fat body as a non-normative body confirms the social stigma of fatness and ensures that more often than not, the fat body is seen as diseased and as a sign of an individual's failure – moral or otherwise.

I am interested in both public and academic discourses about fatness (or obesity) from the beginning of this millennium onwards. I have chosen this particular time frame, because at this point there was a notable change in these discourses. From that point on, the dominant form it has taken is the aforementioned "obesity epidemic discourse" (e.g. Boero 2012; Gard and Wright 2005). Of particular interest here is the cultural and ideological basis of the obesity epidemic discourse: in other words, the social, political, and economic conditions that have produced and maintained it.

To pursue this, I will build on the work of a number of researchers – for instance, Cheek (2008, p. 981), Guthman and DuPuis (2006), Harrison (2012, pp. 330–331) and LeBesco (2011) – who have analysed the connections between fatness, the obesity epidemic, and neoliberalism from different angles in their works. The connection between a hegemonic neoliberal rationale in society and the emergence of the obesity epidemic discourse has already been discussed, for example, by Guthman and DuPuis (2006). I share their view that it can be traced back and essentially linked to the "global" rise in neoliberal economic policy, and the concomitant neoliberalisation of culture. With this in mind, the obesity epidemic discourse can be approached as an exercise in neoliberal biopower, biopolitics, and governmentality.

In fact, the obesity epidemic discourse can be seen as a way that neoliberal governmentality has been introduced into thinking, living and experiencing not just the fat body, but all bodies (Guthman and DuPuis 2006, p. 437). Bodies are governed in neoliberal culture, among other things, through the medicalisation of fatness, the economisation of health and healthcare, healthism, and (I would argue) postfeminist sensibility (see Gill 2007). As a symptom of the underlying healthist discourse and prevailing neoliberal rationale, the obesity epidemic discourse has reinterpreted fat bodies as unhealthy, immoral, and costly. I propose that it is part of a broader neoliberal culture of health, and thus it is also part of neoliberal governing of bodies.

I suggest that neoliberal culture produces (or aims to produce) a certain type of embodied subject. This rationale not only has an effect on the way we think about bodies and how the body is experienced, but also on how certain bodies are selected to represent this culture while others are excluded or vilified (e.g. Wingard 2012). Neoliberal rationale seems to add a new discursive layer to the theorisation of the body and fatness, onto which questions of gender, body norms, health, social acceptability, and, morals, among others, are incorporated.

However, I am not only looking to criticise how this neoliberal ideal has been constructed. My thought has also been inspired by Philomena Essed and David Theo Goldberg's (2002) notion of "preference for likeness". Essed and Goldberg (2002) have studied the preference for likeness and the simultaneous weeding out of the non-preferred type. This overall process they have named "cultural cloning". In relation to bodies, "cultural cloning" or "production of sameness" could mean the systemic preference of some types of bodies over others. Essed (2005) has noted that cultural cloning is a method which aims to ensure that privilege and status (in economic, social, and moral terms for both) stay in the hands of those who are considered the culturally "preferred type". In this process, moral judgment and power are inherently present. It could be perhaps suggested that neoliberal culture not only aims to produce its "preferred" type of embodied subjects, but also those it rejects. Furthermore, my intention is to inspect whether those bodies it attempts to reject or cast aside could be in fact essential to its existence and a part of its logics and organisation. This broader constellation of phenomena could perhaps be described as "neoliberal body culture".

Feminist body studies, fatness, and feminist fat studies

The construction of the neoliberal body could well be approached through a number of body-related phenomena that have become a part of day-to-day life for many residents of the West in the twenty-first century. One could count among them the "wellness culture" as a whole (e.g. Cederström and Spicer 2015); trends in exercise and fitness training; the rise of alternative diets; the increasing use of cosmetic surgery (Kinnunen 2008); the technologisation of health and the "quantifiable self" movement (Singer 2011), to mention but a few. Within all these phenomena, however, it was an easy choice to focus on fatness and gender, and specifically women's fatness and the fat female body. Women's bodies are the prime targets of intensive normative control. To begin with, a woman's role, status, and value in society are still determined very much by her body, by the idea that there is a natural gender difference, and by the consequent gender order. A socially acceptable female body will reflect this gender difference, the hierarchy of power between women and men, and what is considered the "proper" kind of femininity. For women, body size is one of the most important, if not the most important, marker of social acceptability (Bordo 1993; Harjunen 2009; Wolf 1991).

The body became a focus of sociological and feminist inquiry in the 1980s, and by the early 1990s there was already a sizeable mass of work that explored the topic (e.g. Bordo 1993; Featherstone 1991 [1982]; Shilling 1993). Since then, there has been much research on how the (gendered) body has been socially constructed. In feminist research in particular, the focus has been on Foucauldian control, regulation, and disciplining the body. More specifically, it has looked at how discourses and discursive practices produce normative bodies; how bodies are governed in this respect; and how different technologies of power produce, for example, gendered embodied subjects (e.g. Bordo 1993; Harjunen 2009).

As already noted earlier in this introduction, even though feminist academics have explored women's body norms extensively, fatness and fat bodies have not figured particularly prominently in this field until quite recently (the past decade). There is plenty of research on body norms and ideals, and on control and regulation of the female body; however, the main focus has been on the ideal of thinness, on the pressure to achieve a thin body, on dieting (e.g. Orbach 1998 [1977 and 1982]; Bartky 1990; Bordo 1993; Wolf 1991), and on the analysis of eating disorders such as *anorexia nervosa* and *bulimia nervosa* (e.g. Hesse-Biber 1996; Heywood 1996; MacSween 1993). Although there have been some notable exceptions such as the works of Marcia Millman (1980) and Charlotte Cooper (1997, 1998), the topics of fatness, the fat body, and the experience of being fat, were for a long time either ignored in academic research or understood only in relation to the pursuit of thinness and dieting.

Cooper (1997, p. 32), for instance, has pointed out the hypocrisy of feminists who seem to acknowledge fatness as a social issue, yet at the same time build on the medical paradigm of fatness as a problem. Similarly, the "cult of thinness" (see Wolf 1991) has been criticised by feminists, yet dieting is expected of fat women and has been normalised (and still is) as the primary way to deal with fatness (e.g. Orbach 1998 [1977 and 1982]). This means that fatness is persistently approached as a temporary and liminal state of embodied being, thus rendering it impossible to consider fatness as a basis for identity or subjectivity (Harjunen 2009, p. 62).

It seems clear that even many feminists consider the thin body to be the normative female body, and fatness a deviation from the norm. Perhaps for this reason, the de-medicalisation or de-pathologisation of the fat body has not been a priority on the mainstream feminist agenda, even though the medicalisation of women's bodies in general has faced criticism. Abigail Saguy makes an interesting observation regarding this in her recent book *What's Wrong with Fat?* (2013, p. 21). She notes how feminist scholars' interest and analysis has concentrated more on how beauty industry, popular culture, and fashion have contributed to the body image and eating problems of women rather than examining how medical research, public health campaigns, and reporting about the obesity epidemic discourse might do the same. As Saguy observes, medical science's approach to body size is not objective, and cultural assumptions concerning body norms shape the production and reception of scientific knowledge too (Saguy 2013, p. 21). This relative silence over the role of biomedicine in determining normative body size seems to suggest that feminists too have accepted, to some extent at least, the assumed objectivity of the biomedical paradigm of fatness. This underlines just how important the medical paradigm of fatness is and how it actually dominates this subject.

Fatness has never been just a medical or health issue: it is also a social, political, and economic issue, as well as a lived personal experience (e.g. Farrell 2011; Harjunen 2009; Huff 2000). However, this complexity was not reflected in the academic literature for a long time. Although fatness was recognised as a social justice and political issue among feminist and fat activists from the late 1960s onwards (e.g. Louderback 1970; Schoenfielder and Wieser 1989 [1983]), academic studies on fatness as a social and political issue only caught up decades later in the early 2000s. There was some previous research of course, but as a topic of sociological study it was not established. For example, when I first began my own academic exploration into the subject of women's fatness, the relevance of studying fat from a social science perspective was not at all self-evident to my academic colleagues. In fact, when I initially proposed woman's fatness as the subject for my doctoral dissertation in the late 1990s, I was told in no uncertain terms by some of my senior colleagues that the topic was trivial, lacked sociopolitical relevance, and thus was not worth studying. Since then, and not least in part due to the rise of the obesity epidemic discourse in the early 2000s, it cannot have escaped anyone's attention that fat bodies and fatness do have a significant social and political relevance after all.

Since the turn of the twenty-first century, there has been a notable upsurge of interest in the study of fatness in non-medical fields in academia, such as the social sciences. The obesity epidemic discourse that started to dominate the discussion from the late 1990s and the early 2000s onwards (Caballero 2007; Gard and Wright 2005; Wykes 2014, p. 2) helped to redefine and construct obesity as a problem. However, at the same time, and most likely due partly to the exaggerations and inaccuracies of the obesity epidemic discourse, a counter-discourse started to emerge in the form of fat studies or critical fat studies (Wykes 2014, p. 2). The emergence of the obesity epidemic discourse therefore galvanised the study of fatness and fat bodies on both "sides" of the field, as it were.

The role of fat activism and the fat acceptance movement has been notable in politicising fatness and bringing it to the research agenda. In the early 2000s, the work of fat activists such as Marilyn Wann, Charlotte Cooper and others helped to spawn the interdisciplinary discipline of fat studies[5] (Wann 2009, pp. x–xi). The development of fat studies has been crucial to the research of fatness and fat bodies in many ways; it has helped to establish fatness as a credible topic of academic study and made space for researchers who wish to explore social, cultural and political (intersectional) aspects of fat as well as provide a community and possibilities for increased networking. Fat studies draws from a range of scholarship, such as feminist, queer, black, and disability studies (Rothblum and Solovay 2009), and thus it shares with them a rootedness in political activism and commitment to social change.

Now, after over a decade of very public global obesity epidemic discourse, it is obvious that fatness and fat bodies do not exist in some kind of biomedical vacuum and outside of society. Fatness is a feminist issue; and it is simultaneously a social, political, cultural, economic, and personal issue among others. Furthermore, it is always intersectional – different hierarchies of power meet in the fat body. Fat studies as an area of study has established itself quickly in academia and is now regularly represented in academic conferences. In fact, in the past decade and a half, fatness has been explored in a range of fields, such as sociology, media studies, art history, literature, law, sports sciences, food sciences, and nutrition (e.g. Boero 2012; Gailey 2014; Guthman 2009; Harjunen 2009; Kyrölä 2014; LeBesco 2004; Murray 2008; Owen 2012; Saguy 2013; Solovay 2000). There is now not only a refereed *Journal of Fat Studies*, but also a *Fat Studies Reader* (Solovay and Rothblum 2009) that defines the field. The rapidly accumulating body of research that is the result of all this proves that fatness is a complex phenomenon that is multifaceted and requires interdisciplinary research. The other glaring conclusion is that many misunderstandings about the origins and nature of fatness and fat people prevail.

The fat body as the target of biopower

In my previous work, I have studied women's experiences of fatness and the discursive powers that construct fatness (e.g. Harjunen 2002, 2004a, 2004b, 2006, 2009). I have been particularly interested in what kind of embodied subjectivity is available and not available for a fat woman and why. I have looked at how fatness and gender intersect; how theories about fatness and fat bodies arise; and which "powers" construct the fat discourse, i.e., the dominant ways of talking about fatness and framing this topic in Western culture in the early twenty-first century. The theoretical starting point of my work has been the Foucauldian idea of the body as a discursive category and social construct that is created, produced, and reproduced in social interaction and through such social practices such as medicine, the healthcare system, school, religion, and the media.

Like many other feminist researchers who study the body, I draw on Michel Foucault's understanding of power. According to Foucault, power is everywhere and everything is a product of power; operating as it does through discourses, knowledge, and what he called "regimes of truth". In Foucauldian thought, power and knowledge are intertwined insofar as power is constituted through knowledge, for example, science, medicine, or religion (Foucault 1990).

Power often works both through and within the body, making it a central site of power. In Foucauldian thought, biopower is that specific form of power which targets the body. Bodies are governed via biopower. The two main technologies of biopower are the disciplinary power, which aims at shaping the body via discipline, and regulatory power, which is associated with control of the population as a whole (Foucault 1990, p. 139). A notable characteristic of biopower is that it often appears as a benevolent and life-affirming form of power; indeed it is often described as a normalising force, acting in the "best interests" of the population, whether that interest relates to health, well-being, or lifestyle.

Power, especially in the form of disciplinary power, is not perceived as "power-over" something. Disciplinary power is a constructive, pervasive, difficult to resist, and normalising force. Normalisation is thus one of the effects of power, but at the same time the exercise of power is itself also "normalised", hidden within institutions and embedded in everyday discourses and practices (Foucault 1979). The goal of disciplinary power is to create "normality" as defined by the hegemonic discourse in question. Normality is held up as the ideal, and the aim of normalising techniques is to produce individuals who have internalised the discipline and thus become "normal" (Foucault 1979). Biopower, therefore, relies on a sophisticated means of controlling the body through increased surveillance and the creation of a self-disciplined individual who strives for, and is rewarded by, normalcy. As Foucault says, the goal is to create "docile bodies" that may be subjected, used, transformed, and improved (Foucault 1979, p. 136). This necessitates careful and constant observation of the body, and knowledge of what body forms are desirable and acceptable.

The fat body is a good example of being the target of biopower and biopolitical action in general, and disciplinary surveillance in particular. The fat (female) body is a site where the powers that are critical to the construction of fatness are played out. These "powers" reside for example in the medicalisation of fatness, in efforts to normalise the fat body, in the stigmatisation of fatness, and in the liminality of the fat body (Harjunen 2009). These powers are also interrelated so that when their effects are combined, the medicalisation, normalisation, stigmatisation, and liminalisation of fatness and fat bodies produce a particular kind of gendered fat subjectivity. Furthermore, these powers are very much part and parcel of the embodied experience of living in the gendered fat body (Harjunen 2009).

The treatment of the fat body in school that I briefly discussed in the introduction exemplifies biopower and how a body that is considered non-normative gets actively shaped into a normative one. In this Finnish school setting, disciplinary power targeted the body directly in the form of measuring, weighing, monitoring, and evaluating the appearance, health, fitness, and performance of the body (Harjunen 2002). Fatness, especially in its pathologised form as obesity, is obviously a target of intense regulation, but this is not just for those who are fat (cf. Guthman and DuPuis 2006, p. 437). It concerns a far greater proportion of the population, as testified by the widespread diet industry with its multibillion-dollar annual profits.

So far in my work, I have looked at the hegemonic discourse of fatness in the West, and explored how that discourse produces fat (female) bodies as diseased, non-normative, or abnormal bodies that are socially stigmatised and positioned as liminal subjects (Harjunen 2009). In a sense, this book is a continuation of my project to map out those powers that contribute to the production of present-day cultural understanding of fatness and fat bodies. I will thus build on my previous work as well as drawing elsewhere from gender studies, intersectional thought, and fat studies.

My research, whilst remaining closely informed by feminist studies at all times, has aimed to take the feminist study of fatness beyond the issues of appearance, beauty ideals, and dieting. It examines fatness not only as a sociopolitical issue, but also as an experience *within* the larger sociopolitical context. My intention has been to expand the scope of research on fatness and to advance understanding of fatness as a gendered and intersectional social phenomenon and experience, because fatness is always intersectional in nature. By this I mean that fatness always interconnects with other social categories and differences. Fat people are never just fat: they are women, men, working class, middle-class, able-bodied, disabled, and come from a number of different ethnicities, for example. These categories and their intersections instil the power of each in their members, and by so doing, also put people in hierarchical power relationships with each other.

In the contemporary fat discourse, social, moral, political, medical, and economic aspects of fatness are interwoven together. The obesity epidemic discourse is one illustration of this. At one and the same time, it can be perceived as medicalising fatness, as indicating what are (and are not) socially acceptable bodies, and putting these in moral terms. Furthermore, it is very much linked to a number of factors, including politics, social policy, health policy, the production of goods and services, and consumption. The fat body is thus at the intersection of various discussions in body politics that deal with the boundaries of what is a socially acceptable and unacceptable body. I see fatness as a discursive category that is created, produced, and reproduced through various social relationships and practices, such as medicine and the healthcare system, school, religion, and the media, which to some degree aim at shaping the body or determining its acceptable boundaries. But at the same time, I see it as the personal experience of living in a fat body that is inevitably shaped by what goes on in these various discourses and institutions.

My approach to the study of the fat body has been influenced particularly by those feminist scholars who have touched upon the relationships between gender, the body, and the economy in their works. Although it has never exactly been mainstream, over the years there has been a somewhat steady flow of feminist studies that have looked at how economic systems and their rationales may play a part in moulding the (gendered) body. Academics from this vein of research who have helped me formulate hypotheses and guided my general research orientation are, for example, Susan Bordo, Beverley Skeggs, and Barbara Sutton. Bordo has studied the effects of capitalism, popular culture, and consumer culture on the female body in *Unbearable Weight* (1993); while Beverley Skeggs has explored the construction and experience of working class femininity in *Formations of Class and Gender* (1997). Meanwhile, Barbara Sutton has examined women's embodied experiences in neoliberal Argentina in *Bodies in Crisis: Culture, Violence and Women's Resistance in Neoliberal Argentina* (2010). Although these authors approach the topic from different perspectives, with the help of different theorists, and even explore different societies (the US, UK, and Argentina, respectively), all of these works deal with relationships between social construction of the body, gender, and economy. The works highlight how discourses on the body are produced, they explore the material conditions that organise said discourses as well as gendered experiences concerning the body. In addition to these writers, I have also been inspired by other academics from the past decade who have either written or touched upon the topics of living with neoliberalism, or on gender, fatness, and the body in the neoliberal economy (e.g. Guthman and DuPuis 2006; Guthman 2011; LeBesco 2010; Sutton 2010; Ventura 2012; Wingard 2012).

Methodology and data

This book is rooted in the Nordic, and specifically Finnish context. Finland is my native country and the primary setting of this book, with many of the examples I use relating to Finland. However, my point of view is clearly not just a Finnish one. Fat is an issue that transgresses national borders, whether we are talking about its status as a health issue (Gard and Wright 2005), prejudices towards it (Gailey 2014; Valkendorff 2014), media representations of fat people (Kyrölä 2014), or the experience of living in a fat body (Harjunen 2009; Owen 2012). Discourses on fatness are global. The obesity epidemic discourse for instance, is a worldwide phenomenon and it has been promoted by powerful transnational actors such as the WHO, and global media, so much of the discourse is most likely familiar and shared in the global North and West. Indeed, the uniformity of the claims that have been made in the name of the obesity epidemic discourse should raise suspicion even in the most susceptible or biomedically minded academic. Today, there seems to be a consensus around the world that fat is bad, and yet there is also a curious "race" to being "the fattest country" in the world as Solovay and Rothblum (2009, pp. 1–2) have demonstrated.

In this book I have used various types of materials. I have used texts that have been produced about obesity and fatness, particularly in Finland in the 2000s. These include public health materials, such as public health and welfare reports, action plans, brochures, and promotional materials; popular media texts about the obesity epidemic; and articles on body culture in general, and diet and weight loss in particular. I have chosen to limit the period of discussion to the past twenty years, since this is the period of most activity concerning fatness.

While writing this book, I have been a member of an interdisciplinary research group that has two different, but thematically adjoined research projects. The first one focuses on the experiences of the working poor, and the other maps out Finnish people's experiences of fat discrimination. I want to mention this although this data was collected at the point when the writing of this book was already nearing completion, and thus incorporating them here was not possible. However, for the purposes of this book, I have been able to use the data as general background information. This means that I have treated it as providing further insight into the aforementioned phenomena rather than as the basis of my analysis. So although this data is only used as background information for this work, and the results of the research will be reported elsewhere, they provided important information and enhanced my understanding of the relationship between poverty, health and embodied experience, and especially the prevalence of discrimination against fat people in Finland, and the diverse forms it takes.

The first set of data was gathered via a research request that was originally published on the website of the University of Jyväskylä, Finland (and which was subsequently published on the project's own Facebook page), in a number of Finnish newspapers, and on trade union mailing lists and websites. In the research request, respondents were called to write about their own experiences of poverty while being employed. In the request, respondents were asked to write about a number of things, including the possible embodied effects of their life situation: stress, tiredness, nutrition, weight issues, exercise, and so on. The questions were open and the space for replying was not limited. Altogether, 174 replies to the request were submitted. The majority of informants were women, 124 out of 174.

The second, very large set of data, was collected with the help of the journalist Anna-Stina Nykänen and the major Finnish newspaper *Helsingin Sanomat*. I was interviewed for the paper as an expert for a long article about fat discrimination in Finland. In the article a Finnish woman who had struggled with her weight throughout her life told her story. Attached to the article, on the newspaper's website, a survey designed by myself and another member of the research group, Dr Terhi-Anna Wilska, was published. Readers who had experiences of fat discrimination were invited to participate in the survey. The survey consisted of background questions, multiple-choice questions, and one open-ended question, with the space for writing freely about their experiences. Response to the article was overwhelming – all in all around 18,000 people filled in the survey. Again, the majority of informants were women.

Discourse analysis is the method that has been used to examine media texts as well as other materials in this study. Public health materials and media articles have been used mainly to gain an overall understanding of the discourse concerning health and healthy bodies versus obesity as an illness and indication of an unhealthy body. Additionally, and in order to become properly immersed in the topic, I interviewed health and exercise professionals who run municipal, publicly funded weight loss programs (in one Finnish city) about their experiences of running them and the contents of their programmes. Finally, I also undertook some autoethnographic research methods by signing up for a private women-only gym for a year (January–December 2014) to get better acquainted with a space of primary importance for women's body culture these days. I did weight training and participated in different classes that were offered there. These included kettle bell, body pump, body balance, pro roller, Pilates, and stretching classes. During my year at the gym, I also consulted with a personal trainer on four separate occasions about training programs and nutrition; and, being inspired by Cressida Hayes' (2006) autoethnographic work on Weight Watchers, I also took part in a nine-week-long "weight management" group that met once every two weeks for a total of five times at the same private gym during the autumn of 2014 to acquire direct knowledge on what kind of training, advice, and support was on offer for a fat woman in a commercial gym. I wanted to experience first-hand the "new kind of factory floor", as British investigative journalist Jacques Peretti called such a gym in the second episode of his 2013 documentary, *The Men who Made us Thin*.

Since the obesity epidemic discourse originated in the US and many of the components of neoliberal society that affect the body have been most acutely visible there, (food production and consumption, consumer culture in general, beauty industry, fitness and dieting culture etc.), I wanted to spend time there to delve into this cultural reality. During the course of this study, I therefore went to New York City for a six-week stint in the autumn of 2012, and Fort Worth, Texas for eight weeks in the spring of 2015. Among other things, these visits gave me invaluable insights and a wider perspective on the varied social, cultural, and economic factors that influence the way we eat and exercise.

Outline of the book

In each chapter I will explore one aspect of fatness (and the body) in more detail, but these chapters vary in nature. In the first chapters of the book I am building up my case and offering theoretical "building blocks" for understanding the interrelations between body, fatness, gender and neoliberalism. Towards the middle of the book and in the latter chapters, however, the analysis of these relationships moves to the foreground. In the following pages, I will be proposing just one interpretation of the connections and relationships between neoliberalism, fatness, and the body; with the implicit understanding that this is just one of many such interpretations.

In the next chapter, "Neoliberalism, governmentality, and the body", the concepts of neoliberalism, Foucault's concept of governmentality, and neoliberalism as governmentality will be discussed. Governmentality, a concept introduced by Michel Foucault, means a specific way of governing or ruling people, not by sovereign power, but through certain practices or techniques that are designed to shape the subject in a particular way. Neoliberalism can be seen as one such form of governmentality. The processes by which economy affects the body discursively and materially will be examined. To begin with, this will be done in the light of theories concerning the body during the consumer culture of the 1980s. This is because I consider it to be the period when the body maintenance culture, as we know it today, began to emerge. After this, I will examine the "disembodied" economy of neoliberalism and its effects; and finally I discuss intersections of fatness, class and gender.

In the third chapter of the book, "The biopolitics of weight and the obesity epidemic", the medicalisation of fatness will be examined. Further, I will present how the medicalisation of fatness and a neoliberal approach to health seem to complement each other, or at least work in conjunction. I will show how medicalisation helps to construct fatness as a problem that can and should be treated by medical means, even if there are no physical or health problems to treat otherwise. This is one way in which medicalisation functions as a means of normalisation and social and moral control. I will argue here, that the creation of normality within the frame of neoliberal politics is at least as important as the actual goal of good health. The obesity epidemic discourse or the "war on obesity" can thus be seen as an example of a regulatory technique that aims to promote not only health but also normality.

In the fourth chapter, on the economisation of health and the fat body, I will explore the transition from public welfare state healthcare to a neoliberal understanding of health and its consequences. One notable effect of neoliberal governmentality is that health is increasingly understood and discussed in terms of the economy (both in public health bodies and in the media). This extends from the structures of healthcare systems to the individuals. Health has not only become a lucrative business, but the criteria by which the quality of healthcare and health is determined is also increasingly influenced by economic arguments. How does this "economisation of health" affect our understanding of what constitutes a healthy body? In this chapter I will also argue that in the neoliberal frame of healthcare fat bodies have come to be perceived as "expensive bodies". I will further argue that when people are categorised as having "expensive" or "inexpensive" bodies based on their bodily characteristics such as fatness, we are in effect evaluating people's social acceptability, moral competence and "properness of their citizenship" by their assumed "cost" to society.

The fifth chapter, on healthism and individual responsibility, builds on the previous chapters and addresses the concept of "healthism", which sees health as the primary constituent of an individual's well-being, and as something which should be present in all the choices one makes. In this respect, the notion also refers to individual responsibility in these matters. I will argue that the notion of health and healthy bodies that is promoted by healthism is not only exclusive, it also serves a specific function in neoliberal culture: it is the part of neoliberal governmentality that produces certain types of bodies and subjects and rejects others. Here, I will deliberate on the links between healthism and neoliberal governmentality and show how their combined effects reinforce understanding of fatness as an individual's responsibility and enforce the fat stigma. In this chapter, the limits of the responsible self and choice will therefore be explored.

In the sixth chapter, called "Money for your fat!", I will use one particular case to illustrate how health and morals become tangled up with one another in the public discussion on fatness due to the obesity epidemic discourse. I will give a particular example of how fatness is portrayed as wasteful, excessive, unproductive, immoral, and expensive, and how commodification of the body and the global economic discourse are woven into this portrayal. The case I will present is that of a weight loss campaign that ran in Finland in the spring of 2010, some years after the obesity epidemic discourse had spread to Finland. In my view, this campaign provides for an interesting example of the ways in which questions of health, morals, and economics intersect in the discussion concerning fat and fat bodies and how disappearing fat can be exchanged for moral credit.

The seventh chapter, on postfeminism, fatness, and female body norms, is devoted to a discussion on the gendered neoliberal body in the context of (post) feminism. I will build on Rosalind Gill's (2007) claim that postfeminist ideas and perception of the female body seem to draw from and are informed by neoliberal rationality: the emphasis is put on individual responsibility, self-regulation and (apparent) free choice in performing femininity through the body. This chapter aims to shed light on the tangled relationships between postfeminist body politics, neoliberalism and the fat female body.

In the concluding chapter, the results of this book will be summarised and discussed. Medicalisation, healthism, the economisation of health and healthcare, and postfeminist sensibility towards the body together form a very powerful individualising, market-conscious discourse that seems to aim at producing separate, self-governing subjects. Some of the excluding and marginalising effects of the discourse will be discussed.

Notes

1 In this work, the terms fat and fatness are used instead of such terms as "overweight" or "obese". The term "fat" is generally preferred within interdisciplinary and non-medical fat studies literature and among fat activists. The reason for this is that the term "obese" is considered to be a medical term and thus refers to the medical discourse and construction of fatness as a disease, pathology, or as a medical condition. Researchers who approach fatness from critical non-medical perspectives often prefer to use the term "fat", which is considered to be more neutral, descriptive, and non-normative than either "obese" or "overweight". Moreover, during the past decade, there has been a conscious attempt on the part of fat acceptance and fat positive communities, as well as critical fat studies scholars, to reclaim the term fat and imbue it with positive rather than derogatory connotations (see e.g. Saguy and Riley 2005).

2 Although the obesity epidemic discourse has furthered the stigmatisation of fatness, the stigma associated with fatness is by no means a new phenomenon. For example, Farrell (2011) and Huff (2001), who both have explored the history of fatness and shame associated with it (in the Anglo-American context), trace the birth of the fat stigma to the mid-nineteenth century.

3 In the Foucauldian sense of those powers transmitted and produced via discourse, e.g. Foucault 1990, pp. 100–101.

4 The concept of "liminality" was first used by social anthropologist Arnold van Gennep (1960 [1909]) in his study concerning the rites of passage. Nowadays, liminality is often

used in a broader context as a conceptual tool to describe and examine experiences or social statuses that fall somehow between classifications or are otherwise difficult to grasp, explain, or measure. In the context of my research, liminality refers to this experience of being in-between. I argue that fatness is constructed as a transitory and liminal space and experience.

5 A description of fat studies written for the fat studies panel held annually at the PCA/ACA national conference in the US for about a decade now, frames its task and depicts its mission as follows:

> Fat Studies is an interdisciplinary, cross-disciplinary field of study that confronts and critiques cultural constraints against notions of "fatness" and "the fat body"; explores fat bodies as they live in, are shaped by, and remake the world; and creates paradigms for the development of fat acceptance or celebration within mass culture. Fat Studies uses body size as the starting part for a wide-ranging theorization and explication of how societies and cultures, past and present, have conceptualized all bodies and the political/cultural meanings ascribed to everybody. anging theorization and explication os are inscribed with the fears and hopes of the particular culture they reside in, and these emotions often are mislabeled as objective "facts" of health and biology.ogy.d explication os are inscribed with the fears and hopes of the particular culture theye as fundamental and world-shaping as other identity constructs analyzed within the academy and represented in media.
> (http://pcaaca.org/fat-studies/ accessed 1 July 2015)

2 Neoliberalism, governmentality, and the body

From neoliberalism to neoliberal governmentality

Neoliberalism started out as an economic philosophy and an offshoot of liberal economic theory in the 1930s. Today neoliberalism is usually associated with the Chicago school of political economy represented most notably by Milton Friedman (e.g. Brown 2003). Neoliberal economic policy emphasises the role of the free market and the private sector, while pushing for market-friendly policies and a reduction in size of the public sector. Neoliberal economic policy really came to prominence under Thatcher (UK) and Reagan (US) in the 1980s. Since then, neoliberal economic policy and its rationalities, discourse, and practices have been actively promoted and progressively adopted in the Western world and beyond (Harvey 2007).

David Harvey, one of the foremost academics writing about neoliberalism today, has described neoliberalism as follows:

> Neoliberalism is in the first instance a theory of political economic practices that proposes that human well-being can best be advanced by liberating individual entrepreneurial freedoms and skills within an institutional framework characterized by strong private property rights, free market and free trade.
>
> (Harvey 2007, p. 2)

In present-day sociopolitical discussions, neoliberalism is often seen as an economic policy that promotes anti-egalitarianism and furthers social inequality. Neoliberal economic policy is seen as a main reason for the widening income gap between the poor and wealthy globally and locally; for the dismantling of the welfare state or welfare state policies (depending on the context); and for the exploitation of Third World economies (Brown 2003, pp. 3–4). As Johanna Oksala has noted, in the eyes of those who wish to defend a more egalitarian notion of society, neoliberalism appears to be an immoral and callous economic policy, which is not in the slightest bit concerned about the plight of the people it uses to make its profits (e.g. Oksala 2013).

As was already considered briefly in Chapter 1, however, neoliberalism is discussed in more than just the economic context. Neoliberalism is mentioned in politics, the media, academia, and in other public discussions. In recent years, a great deal has been written about the subject in the social sciences and humanities, particularly in the Anglo-American academic context. It has been claimed that there has not only been, generally speaking, a "neoliberal turn" in society (Brown 2003, p. 7) over the past few decades, but also in academic research (Oksala 2014). Neoliberalism has become a popular theoretical lens through which to examine present-day social life in both the domestic and international context; and so its influences, ideology, and policies have been examined in a wide variety of social contexts.

These contexts are, for example, neoliberalism as an economic theory and economic policy (Harvey 2007); as a cultural structure or culture (Ventura 2012); and as a form of governmentality (Brown 2003; Guthman and DuPuis 2006; Lemke 2001). The somewhat heterogeneous understanding of what is meant by neoliberalism, caused by this plethora of contexts, has caused some frustration to the extent that some already see it as a fashionable buzzword, or an empty signifier (e.g. the "Kill this Keyword?" panel at the 2014 American Studies Association annual meeting). In other words, some see that the concept has become dissociated from its original substance (cf. Davis's (2008) discussion on intersectionality as a feminist buzzword). While it might be true that neoliberalism as a concept is increasingly hard to pin down these days, its frequent and diverse use indicates that the framework it offers for analysis nevertheless seems meaningful and current. Indeed, it seems clear that we do not live in a post-neoliberal world; if anything, it has been argued that it is in the nature of neoliberalism to continually extend itself to new fields of life (Brown 2003; Ventura 2012). The forms and manners of this globally dispersed neoliberalism are thus diverse, and as long as its effects are being felt in new arenas, finding new ways to understand its significance in those arenas seems justified.

Governmentality and neoliberal governmentality

Governmentality, a concept developed by Michel Foucault most notably in the lectures he gave at the Collège de France in the 1970s, refers to a regulatory form of power that takes many forms (e.g. Foucault 1991 [1978]). Lemke (2001, p. 11) has observed that the "government" in governmentality refers to a wide range of practices, from political government to self-regulating practices, which Foucault discusses as "technologies of the self". As Foucault (in Faubion 1994, p. 217) himself notes, the purpose of governmentality is to increase the welfare of the population by "the improvement of its condition, the increase of its wealth, longevity, health".

In the same Collège de France lectures, Foucault developed his genealogy of neoliberalism, and consequently, of "neoliberal governmentality". In Foucauldian thought, neoliberal governmentality refers to a type of governing that is permeated by the market (e.g. Lemke 2001). While governmentality refers to the manner in which the welfare of the population is governed by the state, neoliberal governmentality refers to a style of governing that takes its cues from the market.

This means for example that many of the tasks of government, which were previously the responsibility of the state, have been outsourced to the market. Neoliberal governmentality relies on the market to provide services, while at the same time emphasising the individual's own responsibility and control; i.e. the individual must be self-governing in that market (e.g. Guthman 2009). When governing the state is so enmeshed with neoliberal capitalism, the individual's role becomes increasingly perceived as one of consumer and entrepreneur.

Wendy Brown (2003) and Johanna Oksala (2013) among others have written about neoliberalism within the Foucauldian frame of governmentality and have come to similar conclusions about the intertwined nature of economy and other social institutions. Brown (2003, pp. 3–4) notes that it would be misguided to understand neoliberalism as just a set of economic policies that have "inadvertent political and social consequences". Brown continues that within neoliberalism there is a "political rationality that both organises the economic policies and reaches beyond the market". Brown describes this rationality within neoliberalism as a form of governmentality (2003, p. 4), and writes of the wide-reaching nature of neoliberalism:

> Neo-liberalism carries a social analysis which, when deployed as a form of governmentality, reaches from the soul of the citizen-subject to education policy to practices of empire. Neo-liberal rationality, while foregrounding the market, is not only or even primarily focused on the economy; rather it involves *extending and disseminating market values to all institutions and social action,* even as the market itself remains a distinctive player.
>
> (2003, p. 7)

Johanna Oksala (2013, p. 34) also perceives neoliberalism as a form of governmentality in the Foucauldian sense and notes that this underlying political rationality must be taken into account if we are to fully understand the properties that constitute neoliberalism. At the heart of this political rationality is a fudging of the boundary between the economic and social, and an expansion of the market rationality to all aspects of social life (Oksala 2013, p. 34). Market values become the dominant values, and not only in the market. Anything, whether measurable or non-measurable, can be seen through its lens and treated according to its "laws". Everything can thus be economised. Wendy Brown further explains neoliberalism and its "economisation of everything" in a recent interview as follows:

> I treat neoliberalism as a governing rationality through which everything is "economized" and in a very specific way: human beings become market actors and nothing but, every field of activity is seen as a market, and every entity (whether public or private, whether person, business, or state) is governed as a firm. Importantly, this is not simply a matter of extending commodification and monetisation everywhere—that's the old Marxist depiction of capital's transformation of everyday life. Neoliberalism construes even

non-wealth generating spheres—such as learning, dating, or exercising—in market terms, submits them to market metrics, and governs them with market techniques and practices. Above all, it casts people as human capital who must constantly tend to their own present and future value.

(Brown in Schenk 2015)

It is particularly this understanding of neoliberalism as governmentality – which gives neoliberalism the capacity to go beyond economics (while still keeping its economic core), and allows it to seep into so many other fields of life – that makes the concept a relevant framework for my work here. In addition to Wendy Brown and Johanna Oksala's thoughts on governmentality and neoliberal economy, I have also drawn from Patricia Ventura's work (2012) on neoliberal culture. Whereas Brown (2003, p. 7) and Oksala (2013, pp. 32–52) see neoliberalism as a specific political rationality, Ventura (2012, p. 2) organises her understanding of neoliberal rationality within the framework of "neoliberal culture".

In the book *Neoliberal Culture: Living with American Neoliberalism*, Ventura (2012, pp. 2–4) proposes that we should now talk about a "neoliberal culture" not just a neoliberal economy. She sees neoliberalism as a form of governmentality, but is not only interested in neoliberalism as a mode of governing. Ventura aims to understand the ways by which American neoliberal rationality expands and extends from the economic realm to the cultural realm. She approaches neoliberalism as a cultural structure: a framework that organises itself as a "cultural logic" and a "structure of feeling". Ventura proposes that understanding neoliberalism in terms of the structure of feeling, a concept that originates in the work of Raymond Williams (1978, pp. 131–132, in Ventura 2012, pp. 2–3), helps to understand the element of "irresistibility" (for lack of better words) of neoliberalism and explains how it has become an all-pervasive presence in the everyday lives of Americans. As Ventura notes:

> Neoliberalism as a structure of feeling is not merely an economic perspective, not merely a rationality, but it's the concatenation of them. Neoliberal culture as a structure of feeling impels us to extend the market, its technologies, approaches and mindsets into all spheres of human life, to move the ideology of consumer choice to the center of individual existence, and to look to ourselves rather than social-welfare structures of society as the source of our success or the blame of our failure ilure strto define success and failure in market terms. In short, to become entrepreneurs of ourselves as Foucault terms it.
>
> (Ventura 2012, p. 2)

Ventura (2012) makes it clear that her analysis specifically concerns the United States; however, it would seem that the majority of elements she names as characteristics of American neoliberal culture – namely biopower, corporatocracy, globalisation, and the erosion of the welfare-state – are recognisable developments elsewhere too. Of the characteristics she lists, only "hyperlegality" would be difficult to apply in the Finnish context currently, due to differences in the respective countries' legal systems. However, in a globalised world, these other "components" that Ventura identifies as parts of American neoliberal culture, for the large part, are applicable to other Western capitalist societies such as Finland too.

My interpretation is that Ventura taps into a slightly different aspect of neoliberalism than Brown or Oksala, although their interpretations are akin to each other in that they all view neoliberalism as a form of governmentality. They all aim to understand how neoliberalism has got "under our skin", so to speak, and how neoliberalism has become a part and parcel of our everyday lives. Neoliberalism understood as a political rationality that is governmentality explains how we are governed and ultimately learn to govern ourselves, whereas Ventura's notion of "neoliberal culture" puts emphasis on the change that neoliberalism has brought along and that has taken place in everyday structures and cultural representations and consciousness. She examines those elements of neoliberalism that are present in our daily lives that entice us to see and think of ourselves in market terms.

These approaches I have presented above seem to complement each other and together provide a conceptual framework for my project here. Like Brown, Oksala, and Ventura, I too approach neoliberalism as more than just a set of market-friendly policies in politics and economics. For the purposes of this book, I interpret neoliberalism firstly as a form of political rationality or governmentality that has infiltrated many (if not all) areas of our public and private lives, and is increasingly taking over our bodies too (or has already done so). I am particularly interested in the biopolitical (whole population) and the self-governance (individual) aspects of neoliberal governmentality, and in how our bodies have become or are becoming governed by neoliberalism both externally and internally, and are compelled to act along. However, my approach and interpretation has been influenced by Ventura's understanding of neoliberalism as "neoliberal culture" in that I see neoliberalism also more broadly as a cultural phenomenon and setting, not only as a form of governmentality. Thus, I will ask how neoliberalism has become an integral part of our lives, and how it has begun to steer the way we think about, move, and experience our bodies. All of this serves the purpose of inspecting how the "neoliberal body" comes into being. In the following chapters, I will look into the medicalisation of the fat body, the obesity epidemic discourse (OED), the economisation and commercialisation of health, and healthism, among others and examine how these participate in the production of the neoliberal body.

Consumer culture and the body as a "project"

It could be claimed that a particular neoliberal governmentality regarding the body started to emerge or become more visible at around the same time as neoliberalism as an economic policy began to make itself felt in the Anglo-American context in the late 1970s and the early 1980s. A number of changes that seem crucial to the development of present-day body culture took place in the course of the 1980s and 1990s. Among these were the growing emphasis that was put on the appearance of the body, and the newfound popularity of various body maintenance and self-governing practices (Bordo 1993; Featherstone 1991 [1982]), as well as the rising trend of health consciousness and the notion that individuals should be ultimately considered responsible for their health (Crawford 1980). Significantly, a growing interest in sociological research of the body coincided with these developments.[1] In this section, I will briefly discuss 1980s consumer culture and its role in reshaping conceptions of the body, health, and body maintenance. Specifically, my purpose is to shed light on the role of capitalist consumer culture in the discursive production of the body, and the effect it has had on present-day body practices.

The history of body maintenance clearly goes back further than the last forty years, as we can see for example from Turner's (1991 [1982]) analysis of the discourse on diet, which he dates back to the seventeenth century. In the post-war era, capitalist culture had shifted away from manufacture towards consumption, which meant that the role of the individual in that system shifted likewise towards being more of a consumer (Featherstone 1991 [1982], p. 172). What makes the 1980s and early 1990s particularly interesting as a period, however, is that the public and the market's interests regarding the body started to become more and more entangled with each other, and this had repercussions also at the level of individuals and their bodies.

British sociologist Mike Featherstone and American philosopher Susan Bordo are among those academics who connected the 1980s and early 1990s discourse of the body directly to the workings of capitalism. In their respective works, they explored the body in the context of consumer culture and recognised and discussed the effects of its brand of capitalism in relation to body image, body maintenance, and the gendered social construction of the body. Both Bordo (1993) and Featherstone (1991 [1982]) saw mass media, advertising, film, and other popular cultural products as having a key role in promoting certain types of bodies as beautiful, desirable, or socially acceptable. This heightening in the importance of body appearance also coincided with a growing interest in body shaping practices. The desirable body of consumer culture is good-looking (in a normative way), physically fit, youthful, and healthy. It is important that "the look" that is marketed as desirable can be purchased from the market. Capitalist consumer culture creates products that are marketable and consumable, whether these products are goods, services, or images. In consumer culture, the individual is encouraged to work on the body and strive for the image that consumer culture has created as desirable; thus connecting the hard work of body maintenance with pleasure and self-expression.

Featherstone (1991 [1982], p. 170) says that consumer culture invites individuals to look for instrumental strategies to combat "deterioration and decay" of their bodies and combines it with the notion that the body is a "vehicle for pleasure and self-expression". In this manner, the body is portrayed in two conflicting ways: body maintenance work, especially when associated with consumption, is seen as a source of pleasure and hedonism, but at the same time, it is also a means of biopolitical regulation and control. Body maintenance work is conveyed as pleasure-inducing for the individual at the same time as the body is in fact being regulated and governed. This governing of the self that takes its cues from capitalist consumer culture is an illustrating example of neoliberal governmentality (e.g. Guthman 2009).

Featherstone also observed a notable change in the way the body is understood in consumer culture. The body becomes understood as something alterable by the individual if enough effort and body maintenance work is applied. Shilling's (1993, p. 4) later description of the body as a personal "project" seems to be akin to Featherstone's notion of the body's adjustability. Understanding the body as a "project" further highlights the individual's responsibility over the body, whether it is a question of appearance, health or performance.

Featherstone (1991 [1982], p. 171) suggests that, in consumer culture, the body is depicted in terms of an inner and outer body. The inner body represents maintenance and repair concerns over health, illness, and ageing, while the outer body represents the "body's appearance and the movement and control of the body in social space". He concludes that these inner and outer bodies are nevertheless conjoined in consumer culture in that attention is paid to the inner body only to enhance the appearance of the outer body (1991 [1982], p. 171). This primacy that Featherstone notes, of the outer body over the inner, helps to explain why the "appearance of health" has become more important than actual health. As long as the signs that are discursively associated with health are there, the body is deemed healthy. The physical body comes to be seen and interpreted as an expression of the individual's inner world, and Featherstone draws attention to the dire implications of this: "With appearance being taken as a reflex of the self, the penalties of bodily neglect are the lowering of one's acceptability as a person, as well as an indication of laziness, low self-esteem and even moral failure" (1991[1982], p. 186).

For instance, fat bodies are deemed automatically unhealthy based on their appearance. Indeed, the abundance of Foucauldian studies on biopower, biopolitics, and governmentality since the 1980s show just how commonplace it has become to treat the body as an important domain of self-government. Although Featherstone's article dates from over thirty years ago, his interpretation of the importance of body work in consumer culture seems astonishingly up-to-date and relevant. The characteristics of consumer culture he recognised in the 1980s can easily be identified in today's neoliberal culture. In fact, I would argue they are even more pronounced, as the logic of the market has spread into many more sectors of society since then, and the connection between the body and the market has only deepened. Perhaps more than ever, the physical, social, and moral body are now seen as being interconnected and overlapping. The plasticity of the body that Featherstone identified resonates strongly with neoliberalism's emphasis on individual responsibility and (consumer) choice. The idea is that everyone can change their body, if they just put enough "effort" into it and have the right products available to achieve this.

Featherstone did not specifically talk about the trend of health consciousness and healthism that was already spreading in the US at the time he was writing, but he does briefly note the connection between commercial body culture, the commodification of body maintenance, and public healthcare and health promotion, the merger of which has later continued with the help of spreading neoliberal economic policy. In his analysis, Featherstone (1991 [1982], p. 170) does note, albeit in passing, that to some extent commercial and public health interests share a common goal regarding body maintenance. Public health promoters, who are worried about the general health of the population and the spiralling costs of publicly funded healthcare, play along with the body maintenance trend promoted by consumer culture, as it is seen as beneficial, whether or not the motivation behind it might be more cosmetic than to actually improve genuine health. Beauty becomes health, and health becomes beauty, and in the end it is the appearance of health that counts most. By equating health with superficial health, the notion of "good health" becomes increasingly understood in terms of the amount of effort and resources an individual devotes to achieving it. One could even go so far as to argue that neoliberal body culture has actually necessitated obscuring the lines between cosmetic body maintenance and actual health improvement.

Featherstone's observation of this blurring of boundaries between the interests of consumer culture and public health seems to carry even more weight now than in the 1980s, and can be interpreted as an early stage in the spread of neoliberal rationality. He was writing from the British context during a time when the national public healthcare system was still extensive and accessible. The emergence of neoliberal healthcare (and the accompanying privatisation, outsourcing, and prioritisation of certain patients) has entailed the construction of individuals who consider themselves the primary agents of their own health (see, Crawford 1980). Working on the body becomes a matter of choices that are made in the market place. Today this logic of the consumer in the market has spread to public health too.

Obviously body maintenance can be seen as a matter of individual choice to some extent, but the "free" choice over certain decisions concerning the body is limited. For example, both the manner and expected outcome of body maintenance are laden with normative expectations that, among others, are gendered and classed; and in many ways, these assume a type of a subject that is "normal" and thus already privileged. By this I mean that all choices concerning the body are not available for everyone, just as not all choices concerning the body are perceived as acceptable as others. The issue of female body size is a case in point. There are clearly determined gendered norms for acceptable body size (Bordo 1993) and diverging from that norm can have dire consequences, ranging from different types of discrimination to outright harassment and even violence.

It seems evident that those with a body seen as undesirable or unacceptable are given less choice over decisions concerning that body. Moreover, if somebody's physical appearance signals that they are not "choosing" to engage in practices that are deemed beneficial, or choosing the "wrong" methods for their body project, social penalties in one form or another are likely to follow (e.g. Featherstone 1991 [1982]). The individualist body discourse – in the form of the "body as a project" – is clearly complemented by biopolitical concerns. One goal of body maintenance is undoubtedly to produce individuals who have internalised the "duty" to work on the body and who "independently" strive for the ideal of being a responsible and "proper" citizen. For example, the present-day "healthist" discourse not only builds on the idea of choice concerning one's own body, but at the same time encourages us to think about other individuals in our society as responsible for their bodies looking or performing normatively. The individual's choice is therefore tangled up with normative and regulatory body politics, so that body shaping comes to be increasingly seen in terms of morals and duty. But structural issues should not be overlooked here, the neoliberal economy has also brought along with it a growing inequality in income, which in turn means that health as an individual body project has become increasingly exclusive. The body is thus a site of intersectional power relations that have an effect on how the body in question is valued, treated, and experienced in society. Gender, health, and economic status are among the significant characteristics that place bodies in different positions of power, yet by concentrating on the individual all these power positions become easily depoliticised. Individual bodies are parts of a bigger whole, moulded by sociopolitical and economic forces that are usually beyond the individual's control.

The disembodied social analysis of the neoliberal economy

The ties between the economy and the body are numerous and complex; bodies are both materially and discursively constructed and produced by the economic conditions and the economic approach that prevail in the society in which they exist. Economy in its various guises, for example, in the form of physical and material conditions, policies, or a rationale, shapes the way that we understand and theorise about the body. It also has an impact on the material body and the embodied experience of individuals. I have above highlighted briefly the advent of the present-day notion of the body and body culture that relies on and pushes individuals towards self-governing. Neoliberalism is thus not only present in our lives as discourses, or in the manner bodies are governed, but it also has a significant material impact on bodies in everyday life. I will now look more closely at how the neoliberal economy actually physically influences bodies.

Barbara Sutton – who has studied the economic dimension of the body in her book *Bodies in Crisis* (2010) – notes that the direct effect of the economy on the (gendered) body is somewhat rarely examined in the social sciences or feminist research on the body, even though it is clear that bodies are inevitably influenced by the economic climate that prevails. Sutton (2010, p. 62) states that the "economy is not something "out there"; it is not abstract or with little relevance to the body, but a force that is actively shaping bodily experiences and consciousness".

The economy is not only "transported" into the body in the form of discourse, but also in more material ways. It becomes part of the body via the structures and institutions of society, politics and policymaking. Both the individual and macro-level economy have consequences, whether we are talking about the body's appearance, grooming, nutrition, health, functionality, abilities, competences, and life experiences. For example, food security, the ability to acquire adequate and nourishing food; free or reasonably priced healthcare services and medication; and access to education are all not just social but economic questions too and they all shape and manifest themselves in the body.

Those affected by the neoliberal economy and its policies are all embodied human beings (Sutton 2010). And yet, as Sutton has pointed out, the material body is rarely analysed in direct connection with the economy, and so people's experiences of the bodily effects of the economy often remain unexplored, or they are spoken about in such an abstract manner that the body is rendered invisible. More commonly we rely on numbers and statistical analysis to explain these connections. For instance, there is plenty of research looking at the correlation between health and socioeconomic status; that is, how wealth correlates with health, and poverty with ill-health (e.g. Palosuo *et al.* 2009). There are numbers to show how fatness is more prevalent in lower socioeconomic groups (e.g. Stunkard and Sorensen 1993), for example, and how fat women are paid lower salaries than their thin counterparts (e.g. Härkönen and Räsänen 2008). This knowledge about the prevalence, correlation and causation of certain key social factors that affect our bodies' experience and well-being is certainly important, but we learn very little from this of the embodied subject's actual experience of being either fat, female, or poor.

Barbara Sutton (2010, p. 38) has argued that this reliance on "disembodied analysis" of the social world is typical of neoliberal global capitalism. Numerical and statistical data in the form of numbers, indexes, measures, figures, budgets, and profits (i.e., "objective" data) are used to depict the social world by effectively hiding the embodied subject and their experiences (pp. 39–40). So while the above research results tell us that wealth, illness, and gender are certainly connected, they remain quite abstract, and do not tell us anything more concrete about the various problems of these people. Very concrete problems – such as hunger, poor nutrition (and the illnesses that follow from it), and difficulty in getting from one place to another – turn into abstractions that hide the materiality of the body. As a result, the experiences and needs (or possible suffering) of the body are not always adequately recognised; the objective numerical measures are able to hide human suffering (Sutton 2010, pp. 39–40). A disconnect therefore exists between the numbers and what those numbers actually signify in people's lives. The materiality of the body and its experiences and needs are thus ignored, or anyway deemed less important in the analysis than more "objective" data.

Disembodied economic analysis puts the focus on quantifiability, measurability, and cost–benefit analysis of the body. It makes it much easier to make political and economic decisions, but precisely because it is disembodied, it can actually have negative effects on our physical well-being (especially if those policies involve the body)! Put another way, quantitative analysis can be more easily used to justify decisions and policies because the embodied experiences of those people affected by policies are seen as too subjective and hard to quantify. The effects of this, however, may well mean not only increasing the stigmatisation of or discrimination against certain groups of people, but also lowering their quality of life. This is not to deny the usefulness of statistical data or quantitative research, but numbers can only go so far to explain the social realities people live in and their effects on the body. This goes for both understanding fatness as a social phenomenon and as an experience. For example, statistical information about the prevalence and costliness of fatness tell us very little about the lived social conditions that produce fatness, or choices people can actually make regarding their body, how effects of the economy are gendered and how people experience and cope with them.

The body as an intersection of fat, class, and gender

It is often possible to determine the economic status of individuals from the physical appearance of their bodies. The body has always borne messages of status and class that have varied depending on the time and place, but have nonetheless always been present. A body's shape, size, height, and posture, the health of skin and teeth, and so on all convey information about the social position of the said body. Financial, as well as other resources for taking care of one's body, leave their mark on it in a material form (Sutton 2010). The body always communicates something about the society and day-to-day social conditions it is living in, so the body also becomes a sign, symbol, or a representation of its environment. For example, it reflects society's chosen economic policies, and its readiness to invest in its citizens' health, general well-being, social security, and education. Bodies are in many ways manifestations of the conditions of their particular past and present: they reflect their abilities, the resources available to them, and the way they are treated. Investment in health and welfare policies will have accumulated in the body over years, decades and generations. In particular, longstanding good (or poor) health will be visible in people's bodies. Neoliberal policies leave their mark on the body in many different ways. For example, the cutting of funding in Argentina (Sutton 2010, pp. 37–38) has led to poor or insufficient nutrition, unsafe housing, and lack of free or reasonably priced healthcare and medication, which have all taken their physical toll on the bodies of those who rely on them in the long run (if not immediately).

Latent (if not blatant) inequality is an inherent part of the neoliberal economy (e.g. Brown 2003; Oksala 2013). And, as Sutton (2010, p. 35) says, "[s]tructures of inequality, including economic disparities, are embodied". Sometimes the signs of power and oppressive practices can thus be read directly off the bodies in signs of malnutrition, ill health, harmful beauty practices, and physical violence. Socioeconomic differences and other (im)material means to take care of one's body leave their mark on the material body (e.g. Sutton 2010); and where healthcare and social services are publicly provided, extensive and easily accessible, there is an absence or low occurrence of certain treatable ailments that are otherwise an everyday occurrence in places where such systems are only accessible to those who can pay for them. It has been well-established that social equality correlates with the health and well-being of a society, whereas social inequality and injustice correlate with illness (e.g. Palosuo *et al.* 2009). For instance in Finland, neoliberal erosion of the welfare state and its policies has affected the most vulnerable groups of people first and has clearly aggravated social inequality (Riihelä *et al.* 2002). One's health status has started to correlate with one's socioeconomic status. The wealthier one is, the healthier one is; health has become more of an issue of socioeconomic class again (e.g. Berg 2010; Erola 2009; Palosuo *et al.* 2009).

In the present-day neoliberal economy, the effects of the economy on the body are varied and multilayered.[2] They not only depend on socioeconomic divisions though; other social divisions and hierarchical power relations play a vital role too. In short, the economy affects different bodies in a variety of ways. Bodies are always gendered, racialised, ethnicised, and sexualised, among other things; and so what they are capable of, allowed to be, and so on, also affects their economic position in these contexts. Furthermore, various inequalities will interact with each other so that relationships between the body and the economy are in fact intersectional, and therefore even more specific than would otherwise be the case. I thus recognise the multiplicity, intersectionality, and specificity of inequalities; and with this in mind, the systems of inequality that are approached here will be primarily those of class, gender, and body size. The body can therefore be seen as an expression of a complex set of economic, social, and political criteria. And, lest we forget, it is both a consequence of the material conditions and resources available to it (e.g. wealth, education, geographical location) as well as a symbol of them (e.g. the body is a marker of social status/class/education/origins).

Fatness is commonly associated to other hierarchical intersections of power, such as gender and socioeconomic class. The social status of the fat body is low, while thinness is seen as a marker and prerequisite for class status (Guthman and DuPuis 2006). It has been well documented that the stigma of fatness is especially established for women, as it is connected to gendered expectations of normative body size, shape, and appearance (e.g. Harjunen 2009; LeBesco 2004). Furthermore, social class is gendered and embodied (LeBesco 2007). Käyhkö (2006) who has written about Finnish working-class girls' experiences, and Skeggs (1997) who explored British working-class girls experiences, have concluded in their respective works that the gendered body plays a key role when working-class girls are taught about social class.

Fatness is classed demographically, and is more common in lower socioeconomic groups (Palosuo *et al.* 2009). But the fat body has also become a sign of lower class status, especially in combination with other intersections of power. The combined stigmas of fatness, being female, and being poor have been observed, for example, by LeBesco (2007). Skeggs (2005) too has noted that the fat female body has begun to signify the deviant, the ignorant, and the body of an underclass that represents the "moral opposite" of the middle class body and the "normal" middle-class values attached to it. Herndon (2005) has observed how fatness often works as an exacerbating additional stigma for people who are already being marginalised for some other reason. Thus, attempts to control fatness often target people who are already being controlled anyway. Power relations embedded in these social statuses are all part of the issue of fatness; not only how fat is presented, constructed, and experienced, but ultimately also how fat people are treated.

Transgression of the normative boundaries of body size is especially critical for women. Thinness is a loaded signifier and has come to signify in many cases overall social success. It is a sign of health, social acceptability, appropriate femininity, middle-class values, and having a sexually desirable body. Connecting social acceptability to a body size that is unattainable for many inevitably constructs a system of privilege and exclusiveness. It is no exaggeration to claim that today, in the neoliberal context, thinness is identified as a privileged and exclusive position. As a result of the intersectional effect of gender and fatness, fat women are, for example, frequently discriminated against in the labour market. Body size is in itself an economic question for women, and a body size that is deemed "wrong" poses an economic risk for women in particular. A fat body may thus automatically assign a woman to a lower class status in spite of her qualifications (e.g. Kauppinen and Anttila 2005). At the same time, fatness and socioeconomic status are also intertwined in a vicious circle so that fatness produces lower socioeconomic status and likewise lower socioeconomic status produces fatness (e.g. Stunkard and Sorenson 1993). In this respect, fat women are often paid lower salaries, their career paths are rockier, and they are more frequently unemployed than their thin counterparts (Härkönen and Räsänen 2008; Kauppinen and Anttila 2005). In fact, a Finnish study found that especially highly educated fat women were discriminated against in working life, and that there was actually a significant wage gap between fat women and their normative-sized counterparts (Sarlio-Lähteenkorva, Silventoinen, and Lahelma 2004).

It is no coincidence that fatness as a phenomenon intersects with gender and social class. The fat body is obviously classed, and today it is often associated with lower social class status in individualist societies (Herndon 2005; Skeggs 2005). Whereas fatness was previously associated with wealth and a certain over-indulgence of the rich (Farrell 2011), it is now increasingly connected to poverty, low social status, and the alleged immoderation of the poorer classes. While moral condemnation of "fat cats" stems from their perceived privileged position and power, fatness that is a product of being underprivileged is just seen as an individual's moral failure. Fatness and lower class status are both constructed as a matter of the individual's choices and personal "bad" behaviour (e.g. McKenzie 2015, pp. 10–12). Fatness has thus, in itself, become a representation and sign of lower class status.

Notes

1 According to Shilling (1993, p. 35) four major social factors provided the context for the rise of body studies in sociology: (i) second wave feminism; (ii) demographic change (i.e., an ageing population); (iii) a change in the structure of modern capitalism with the burgeoning of consumerism; and (iv) a crisis in understanding the body.
2 Bodies are not only shaped by their local circumstances; in the global neoliberal economy bodies are also locally affected by global flows in the economy, as demonstrated for instance by Brown (2003) and Sutton (2010).

3   The biopolitics of weight and the obesity epidemic

As we have seen so far, fatness is a characteristic or condition that is largely defined by biomedical discourse. Consequently, fatness has been seen as primarily a health issue and a medical problem, which can and should be solved by medicine. Due to its medicalisation, the fat body is thus rarely approached in terms of physical diversity or variation; instead it has been constructed as pathological and suffering from a disease known as "obesity". It is this biomedical construction of "obesity" and "obese" people that has been the focus of biopolitical interest. Since the turn of the century, the aforementioned "obesity epidemic discourse" (OED) has promoted fatness as the number one health threat in the world. In this chapter, I will discuss the biopolitics of weight and body size; the biomedical paradigm; the medicalisation of fatness and the idea of "normal weight"; and the relationship between fatness and health. I will then talk more about the obesity epidemic discourse and how it has been instrumental in the medicalisation and construction of fatness as a "social disease" and as a "metaphorical illness".

My aim in this chapter is to depict how fatness has been constructed as a medical problem, and the fat body as a non-normative body that itself is seen as the disease. Together with Chapters 4 and 5 – in which I will first discuss the economisation and commercialisation of health and healthcare, and then healthism and individual responsibility – my purpose is to gradually expose each component of neoliberal body culture. My aim is to show how these different but interlinked constituents of the discourse on fatness merge. It is my claim that the above issues have a major role in shaping neoliberal body culture and in determining the role of the fat body in that culture. Above all, they make fatness a question of both individual responsibility and the public economy at the same time.

The biopolitics of weight

Measuring, monitoring, and keeping a record of these measurements are among the typical techniques of biopower that governments use to manage and control their populations (e.g. Foucault 1990, 139–141). The overt goal of biopolitical government is to sustain the life of the population by improving its health, preventing illness, and eliminating risks. This duty is usually given to specific national public health institutions or other related governmental agencies.

Body weight is probably one of the most common targets of biopower today. Our bodies become objects of measuring and monitoring from early on. Newborn babies are routinely measured and weighed right from birth and measuring has usually already started while *in utero*. In Finland, for example, one's body size is regularly monitored all through one's life. Mother-and-child clinics meticulously record the child's development from the prenatal phase right through the early childhood years. From then on, children's body measurements are regularly recorded via school healthcare, and later on at regular intervals by student healthcare, maternity care (for expecting mothers), and occupational healthcare. It is fair to suppose that measuring the body is an established part of biopolitical government of the population in Finland today.

Biopower is used to promote the health and well-being of the body, but the same power may also function as the means to control it. Biopower is essentially a normalising force; its goal is to produce normal, standardised citizens and to correct or weed out non-normative or defective bodies (Foucault 1990, p. 144). The standards and limits for normalcy are set by scientific experts, and so in the case of the physical body, normalcy is defined by biomedical expertise. Meanwhile the disciplinary form of biopower aims at creating subjects who have internalised these standards to the extent that they have become self-disciplined subjects (e.g. Foucault 1979).

The regular measuring, monitoring, classifying, and disciplining of bodies serve as techniques by which people are trained to learn the boundaries of the normal body and learn how to monitor these boundaries themselves.[1] In essence, we are systematically taught to think about and evaluate our bodies' normality by criteria set by medical science. As a biopolitical project, learning about acceptable dimensions for the body seems to have been successful. Most people seem to know their "vital statistics", especially their height and weight (Harjunen 2009, p. 31). This basic knowledge of the body is perhaps understood as part of the know-how that is required for the modern day "health citizen" who has internalised the principles of self-monitoring (c.f. Hélen and Jauho 2003, p. 14).

Women in particular are often highly aware of their body's dimensions, and whether their weight is within the normal range or not. In a previous study, I observed that women who have a history of fatness and dieting seem to be able to recount their weight history from year to year, or rather from milestone to milestone to the nearest kilogram, even after many years (Harjunen 2009, p. 31). This is hardly surprising as it has been well established that norms regarding the body's appearance, especially body size, are stricter for women than for men (e.g. Bordo 1993; Gailey 2014; Wolf 1991). Women's body size is culturally monitored more closely, and women are also encouraged to monitor and control their body size much more than men. It is a common experience for women to feel significant social pressure to have a normative-sized body. Furthermore, women are also more heavily penalised for transgressing body size norms (e.g. Gailey 2014; Harjunen 2009). This is partly an effect of the patriarchal organisation of society and the understanding of women's worth defined by their role within it. The intense sexualisation of women's bodies and the exclusive conflation of the slender body with desirability (and social success) in the patriarchal context contributes to women's perceived duty to monitor themselves and govern their bodies[2] (e.g. Bordo 1993; Gill 2007). Biopolitical monitoring and control of body weight and size is thus combined with gendered body norms for women.

Biomedicine and normal body weight

As discussed in the previous chapter, medicine and medical professionals have constructed fatness in the very Foucauldian sense of "discourse" and "power-knowledge" (see e.g. Foucault 1979; 1990). Indeed, medical discourse has dominated both knowledge and knowledge production on fatness. Until the late 1990s, fatness and fat bodies were observed and discussed almost exclusively in the context of medicine and medical knowledge. This has hugely affected the way we think, view, and treat fatness and fat bodies (Harjunen 2009).

Due to its dominance in knowledge production, the biomedical perspective on fatness is generally considered to be the most authoritative, as this authority is based on the fact that scientific research has a reputation for objectivity and neutrality. As a consequence, the biomedical paradigm is now commonly held to be "the truth" in both academic and popular discourses on fatness (e.g. Harjunen and Kyrölä 2007; Kyrölä 2007) and alternative views have often been received sceptically or, at least, are seen as being of secondary importance to the medical paradigm. Analyses and interpretations from other academic fields that challenge this hegemony, such as the humanities, or social and cultural studies, have had to struggle for legitimacy, recognition, and visibility (e.g. Solovay and Rothblum 2009, pp. 6–7).

In the context of biomedicine, bodies that exceed the range determined as normal weight are seen to be ill, or at least at risk of becoming so (Harjunen 2004a; 2009). Methods for measuring and classifying body weight have varied over the course of history. Currently the most common way to distinguish normal from non-normal weight (or healthy from unhealthy) is the body mass index or BMI. Body mass index classifies weight into the following groups: underweight (less than 18.5); normal (18.5–24.9); overweight (25–29.9); obese (30–34.9); severely obese (35–39.9); and morbidly obese (over 40) (The WHO Global Database on Body Mass Index n.d.). Normal BMI means the range where an individual's health should be at its most optimal. Notably, the BMI charts circulated in the media tend to depict overweight categories in more detail than others. Categories of severely underweight (BMI under 16) and very severely underweight (BMI under 15) rarely appear. This perhaps also reflects stronger medicalisation of fatness and its perceived greater problem status.

As a concept "normal weight" is a relatively recent innovation which did not emerge from the field of medicine or healthcare, but from the insurance industry. Statistician Louis Dublin first determined "normal weight" for the Metropolitan Life insurance company in the 1940s. The company needed to know about the mortality rate of its clients and so Dublin set about collecting information on those clients that had lived the longest (Boero 2012, p. 9; Oliver 2006, p. 19).

From this data, Dublin calculated weights that would predict the lowest mortality for different heights. Since Metropolitan Life was most interested in premature deaths, its data collection and charts concentrated on the relationship between weight and longevity. This is the reason why life expectancy became a central factor in determining what was a normal body size (Boero 2012, pp. 8–9; Oliver 2006, p. 18). Normal weight as a category was thus born out of a biopolitical need in part motivated by economic factors. The "Met Life charts" (as they are usually referred to) were soon adopted by the medical establishment to indicate individuals in "optimal health", even though they were originally meant for actuarial, not medical use. Indeed, according to Oliver (2006, p. 19) by the 1950s these charts were already the primary way to determine normal weight in the US.

It is perhaps fitting, therefore, that the BMI itself also originated as a tool of statistics and population control, rather than medicine. In its very first form it was developed by the Belgian astronomer and early sociologist Adolphe Quetelet in the nineteenth century. Quetelet wanted to find out whether the probabilities of certain trends could be predicted from large samples, with his aim being to determine the average size of the (male) body. Quetelet studied conscripts and found that the weight of those men who were closest to the middle of the distribution curve was proportional to their height squared (Oliver 2006, pp. 17–18). This he concluded was "normal" weight, as it was based on the average (statistically) normal distribution (Oliver 2006, pp. 17–18). This began to be used more widely in medicine in the 1970s and soon replaced the Met Life charts that had previously been in use. In Finland, the BMI began to be used in healthcare in the 1980s (Heliövaara and Aromaa 1980).

The BMI has been criticised a great deal for a number of well-known shortcomings. Probably the most familiar of these is its poor ability to separate muscle tissue from fat. Because muscle weighs more than fat, very athletic and muscled people often have high BMIs that exceed the range of normal weight. Based on BMI classification, a fit, muscled individual with a very low fat percentage can be categorised as overweight or obese and therefore unhealthy based on their weight. This happens when just the weight, not the content of that weight, is measured. Moreover, BMI has been found to be an unreliable measure for normal (i.e., healthy weight) among very young or elderly individuals. It is not reliable for different ethnicities or genders either (e.g. Grabowski and Ellis 2001; Wen *et al.* 2009).

Another point of criticism is that normality as defined by the BMI is in part a social construct: it is changeable and a matter of negotiation, and it has been used politically and strategically in the past (Campos 2004; Oliver 2006). A famous example of this is how the normal range of BMI was changed in 1997 in the US. The former upper limit of normal weight on the BMI was lowered from 27 to 25 which meant that millions of North Americans became recategorised as overweight overnight (Oliver 2006; Squires 1998). As a consequence, there were many more people classified as potentially ill that would be in need of services that would help them to get healthy (i.e., lose weight). Shifting the boundaries of normal weight is a classic example of action in which biopolitical health concern seems to meet economic and commercial interest.

Body weight and health

In medical discourse, body weights are classified as normal, at risk, and non-normal. Normal weight is equated with health, and thus by default all the other weights are marked as unhealthy. BMI categorisation enforces the notion that there is causality between certain body weights and good health or illness. The problem is that, while some significant correlations between body weight and certain illnesses have been found, this has been often confused with causation, particularly in popular discourses on fatness, and claims that fatness "causes" certain illnesses are thus an over-exaggeration.

During the past decade in particular, the medical discourse on fatness has come under increasing fire. For example, the medicalisation of fatness has been re-evaluated in terms of the biomedical fat paradigm and the role of political and economic powers in its formation have been brought into discussion and analysed (e.g. Campos 2004; Campos *et al.* 2006; Gard and Wright 2005; Oliver 2006; Saguy 2013), and found to be not as monolithic, unified, or consistent as previously supposed. In recent years, research from both inside and outside the field of biomedicine has revealed inaccuracies and inconsistencies in determining "normal weight", and the effects of fatness on people's health, among other things (e.g. Boero 2012; Flegal *et al.* 2005).

Especially in the light of recent research, it looks like that the relationship between weight, health, and mortality is more complex than has previously been assumed. There is the long line of biomedical research which shows that fatness is a health risk, and a factor that correlates with increased mortality, however, this is not the whole picture. For example, the belief that higher BMI automatically means ill-health has been debunked regularly in recent research. There is also a great deal of ambiguity in the relationship between health and weight as well as between weight and mortality (e.g. Campos 2004; Cogan 1999; Flegal *et al.* 2005; Flegal *et al.* 2013; Wessel *et al.* 2004). It is known that extremely low weights and very high weights are more likely to exacerbate other health issues (e.g. Flegal *et al.* 2007), but in general, the range of weights in which people can remain healthy appears to be broader than the BMI classification currently in use would lead us to believe. For example, there is research that suggests that it is the fitness, not fatness, that counts the most and that it is quite possible to be healthy and fat, if one is physically active (e.g, Lee, Blair, and Jackson 1999). In fact, it has been shown in research that the healthiest people with the lowest mortality are not in the normal weight category (18–25 on the BMI scale), but the overweight category (25–30 on the BMI) , and that it is the underweight and obese (especially very obese) that are most at risk and with the highest mortality (Cao *et al.* 2014; Flegal *et al.* 2005; 2007). People in the normal weight range apparently have a higher risk of cardiovascular disease than overweight people (Romero-Corral *et al.* 2006), while in elderly people a higher BMI seems to correlate with increased longevity (e.g. Grabowski and Ellis 2001).

The possibility that one can in fact be healthy with a weight that exceeds the normal goes very much against the grain of the current hegemonic view of health and weight. This is perfectly captured in the term "obesity paradox", coined to refer to those cases in which a higher BMI actually seems to alleviate or protect people from certain illnesses or their symptoms. For example, patients with a higher BMI have also been shown to recover faster after suffering a heart attack (e.g. Curtis *et al.* 2005; Fonarow *et al.* 2007; Vaughn *et al.* 2014) and to have a lower rate of mortality among kidney dialysis patients (e.g. Kalantar-Zadeh *et al.* 2003; 2007). Nevertheless the existing hegemonic knowledge purports that weight above normal is always detrimental to your health.

In public discussion on fatness, a causal relationship between weight and health is usually presented in a straightforward manner, the message being that "fatness kills". Different results acquired in research concerning the health effects of different weights do little to dispel this in public or academic discussion. The idea that normal weight is the only healthy weight appears simpler to understand and more culturally consistent and definitive, even though it is not necessarily the case. The abovementioned research results are not the only ones that seem to confirm that a person's health cannot be determined by weight alone, and that it is possible to be healthy and fit in many different weight ranges. This calls for other factors to be taken into account rather than just weight, and for a new more representative system of categorisation to be made. One alternative analytical tool that has been developed for the purpose of identifying possible weight-related health effects is the "Edmonton Obesity Staging System" that classifies stages of obesity from zero to five. At zero, the person has no negative health effects relating to weight. The advantage of this system is that it takes into account that it is possible to be healthy and have a higher BMI and that weight is only one of the factors counted as having an effect on health (Sharma and Kushner 2009).

The BMI range for normal/healthy weight currently in use would therefore appear to be too narrow, judging from the research cited above. The categories seem to "leak" quite a bit, and the border between normal and overweight appears to be set too low. It seems that BMI alone is not a reliable measure for health; a person with higher BMI may be even healthier than one whose body weight is within the normal range. And yet, in many cases, we nevertheless choose our understanding of health to be determined by this indicator that is well-known for its flaws and unreliability. This makes the act of using it particularly normative – in fact the wielding of biopolitical power relies on BMI for its normative effect.

This emphasis on the "measurability of health", leads to a very restrictive and normative idea of health and healthy bodies. Johanna Mäkelä and Mari Niva (2009), among others, have argued that obesity played such a central role in the health discussion exactly because it is easily measurable and such an easy target in the medicalised and neoliberally inclined societal climate.

In the biomedical context, normal weight is used as a code for "healthy weight" and healthy weight is used, in turn, to indicate "normal body" size. This leads to the normalisation of dieting as one of the primary ways to "get healthy". In fact, it is commonly assumed that all the health problems of fat individuals are due to their weight (e.g. Cooper 1998; Gailey 2014; Harjunen 2004a), and this might mean that health issues unrelated to weight may go undetected because they are not even looked for properly. Defining weight narrowly through the BMI basically leads to a weight-centric view of health, and a healthcare system that promotes weight loss as a blanket solution for all health issues. Since it is well-known that the long-term success rate of dieting is around 5–6%, which means 95% of dieters fail (Sarlio-Lähteenkorva 1999), encouraging people to get healthy by dieting is basically setting them up for failure – many of those who lose significant amounts of weight, regain it again later.

In this respect, health and weight categories do not really correspond if, for example, "normal" and "overweight" people have practically the same risk of ill-health and mortality. Insisting that all weights exceeding the currently acknowledged normal-weight category pose a similar risk, or that all weights above the normal range are unhealthy, serves a biopolitical purpose. It seems that one reason for this "fat panic" has been because "overweight" and "obese" have been lumped together in the same figures, thus magnifying the scale of the problem. For example, in the latest "Health at a Glance: Europe 2014", a report produced by the OECD and The European Commission, it says that "in the EU, 53% of adults are now either overweight or obese". This makes the figure sound alarming, when in fact further investigation would reveal that only 16.7% of these are obese, meaning that a full 36.3% are simply overweight. So are there any other reasons why these categories might be lumped together, other than to raise public awareness of the health risks of obesity? It has been suggested that the obesity epidemic discourse might be driven more by the ideology of weight loss itself, than by any real health concerns (Boero 2012; Gard and Wright 2005; Rail *et al.* 2010). If that is the case, any amount of weight that exceeds the normal weight is portrayed as a problem. The rest of this chapter will thus look more closely at the "obesity epidemic discourse", and at how this discussion itself has become an epidemic.

The "obesity epidemic discourse" . . . epidemic

Since the early 2000s, fatness has been discussed predominantly within the framework of the "obesity epidemic discourse". Cooper (2010, p. 1022) traces the origin of this concept back to a 1997 World Health Organisation (WHO) report called "Obesity: Preventing and managing the global epidemic". But the actual phrasing "obesity epidemic" was first used in the 2001 text of the US Surgeon General's "Call to Action to Prevent and Decrease Overweight and Obesity" (Mitchell and McTigue 2007, p. 392). Since then, it has been used profusely both in popular and academic contexts around the globe. The obesity epidemic discourse has been promoted in transnational organisations such as the WHO, and national governmental bodies have also helped to legitimise it as the dominant approach to fatness over the past decade.

The obesity epidemic discourse branded obesity as one of the main, if not the most important, health threats in the world today (e.g. Gard and Wright 2005). The obesity epidemic discourse quickly took over both academic and public discussions on fat and brought with it an emphasis on understanding fatness as a medico-social problem with economic–moral overtones. Academic research that diligently promotes the obesity epidemic discourse has also been referred to as "obesity science" (e.g. Gard and Wright 2005; Rail *et al.* 2010).

The obesity epidemic discourse is a unique political phenomenon regarding health and the body, as it has been unusually global in nature. In this respect it could be said that the obesity epidemic discourse itself has spread like an epidemic. Very similar discussions about the causes and effects of obesity, and about its victims and heroes, have gone on simultaneously, for example, in the US, Australia, Finland, Sweden, and the UK (Gard and Wright 2005; Harjunen 2009; Solovay and Rothblum 2009, pp. 1–2).

The uniform subject nature of the obesity epidemic discourse around the world dawned on me during one international fat studies conference I attended in Sydney, Australia in the autumn of 2010. I counted that during the sessions I attended at the conference, researchers from eight different countries reported that their national population was "the fattest" in the world, or in Europe, or in the Nordic countries, and so on. This is just one anecdotal example of rhetoric used in the obesity epidemic discourse, but this kind of hyperbolic language is typical of it, and it is often accompanied by misleading or simply bogus statistics. One of the most famous examples is the report by the US Center for Disease Control (CDC) in 2004, which claimed that 400,000 people die annually in the US from being overweight or obese. This figure was first revised to 365, 000 and then revised again to 25,814 after heavy criticism concerning the methodology – about 94% less than the original figure! (e.g. Campos 2004, p. 17; Flegal *et al.* 2005)

The obesity epidemic discourse made fatness a global biopolitical concern; and as a consequence, fat bodies were scrutinised all over the world. There was now talk of a "war on obesity" which, in itself, goes some way to show how much of it was a biopolitical regulatory technique. Purportedly aimed at promoting health, the obesity epidemic discourse was actually going further to indicate that certain types of embodied experience were innately non-normative. The obesity epidemic has thus functioned as a further rationale for medicalisation of fatness, thus contributing to normalisation and social control.

Medicalisation means the spreading of medical expertise into otherwise non-medical spheres. For example, social issues might become seen as medically treatable (Conrad 2007). Although obesity was originally defined by biomedicine, it has never been just about health. As we have already seen, it is a combination of medical, social, and moral elements. After examining the grounds on which obesity might be considered a purely medical disease, Hoffmann (2015) has suggested that fatness is more like a "social disease". He observes that when compared to traditional biomedical conceptions of disease, fatness does not fulfil these criteria, although obesity can increase the risk of developing an illness. By "social disease" he means that obesity can be defined in terms of those social norms it seems to depart from. Obesity is seen, for example, as a breach of aesthetic ideals and a weakness of will (Hoffmann 2015).

It is this propensity to see fatness as a "disease package" which conveniently lumps the aforementioned increased risks of illness together with aesthetic, moral, and behavioural phenomena which has led to the increasing medicalisation of fatness and been essential for the success of the obesity epidemic discourse. What we are thus trying to cure is not just the alleged health or medical concerns associated with obesity but also this "social disease" too.

Hoffmann's observations seem to confirm what other academics have written about the reasons for treating fatness in the first place (e.g. Gard and Wright 2005; Oliver 2006). Many agree that it is not solely a health matter on either an individual or societal level. Social, political, economic, and moral issues have always had a part to play alongside this, or under the guise of health and well-being (Harjunen 2009). Reservations about the motivation behind the battle against obesity have been expressed, both within and outside the medical community. For example, Fitzgerald (1994) suggested that medicine's battle against obesity could be explained in part by a tendency to medicalise behaviour we do not approve. In their much-quoted editorial in the *New England Journal of Medicine,* Kassirer and Angell noted that the description of obesity as a disease is an "arguable assertion", and that the emphasis on treating obesity seems to be more often about normalising the obese person's body, i.e., weight loss, than on improving the patient's health (Kassirer and Angell 1998, p. 52).

Other issues besides fatness have also been identified as purely medical problems, when in reality they are heavily influenced by prevailing societal values. This is partly because society has not been able to accept certain behaviours, physical and physiological differences, or indeed lifestyles that diverge from the norm. For example sexual orientation, gender identity, and many disabilities have all been medicalised. This means that a large number of people have been considered ill and diseased, because they have broken prevailing social norms in one way or another. The fact that many of these groups of people have been later demedicalised can be taken as a clear indication that medicine is susceptible to changes and shifts in societal norms. Fatness could be understood as one modern day example of this phenomenon.

It is a further sign of the uneasy and complex relationship between fatness as an illness and fatness as a social issue that a medical condition is given for a group of people outside the medical sphere. "Obesity" depicts illness and a non-normative condition from the outset, thus rendering it far more difficult to recognise these people as healthy than would otherwise be the case. Hoffmann's (2015) suggestion that fatness be labelled a social disease would therefore seem appropriate in this sense. The fact that a name of a disease is used to name a group of people, and that it is used in everyday parlance to describe those people, tells us that "obesity" is not considered like other illnesses, but something more than that; fatness is taken as a symbol of a more all-encompassing non-conformity or deviance that exists within the individual. The medicalisation of fatness both functions as a mechanism for producing, reproducing, and maintaining fatness as a socially stigmatised condition; and as a power technique that aims at normalising it.

Moral panic and the metaphorical illness of obesity

A number of researchers have discussed the obesity epidemic discourse in terms of moral panic (e.g. Gard and Wright 2005; Harrison 2012; LeBesco 2010; Campos *et al.* 2006). According to Cohen, who originally coined the term "moral panic", the phenomenon or group of people at the centre of a moral panic is typically simplified and stereotypical, and "defined as a threat to societal values and interests" (Cohen 1972, p. 9). The phenomenon is usually exaggerated, and the information presented is often one-sided and biased. There are a number of theories on the origins of moral panics. Although media often plays a major role, not all episodes of moral panic are created by the media (Thompson 1998, p. 98). Moral panic can begin at the grass-roots level and grow into a public outrage, but it can also be manipulated from above by a range of interest groups and power elites (Goode and Ben-Yehuda 1994). The representation of the phenomenon or the group of people at the centre of moral panic is typically simplified and stereotypical; the phenomenon is exaggerated and information presented is one-sided and often biased. Most importantly moral panic episodes help to create a culture of fear (see Glassner 1999).

All the typical characteristics of a moral panic can be identified in the obesity epidemic discourse (Harjunen 2004: LeBesco 2010). Fatness is considered both a physical deficiency and a character flaw. Representations of fat people are highly stereotypical and public discussion on fatness has been, and continues to be, prejudiced, simplistic, and often downright misleading. It seems that the moral panic over fatness has followed the general pattern of moral panics about other issues. In the first phase highly exaggerated figures of mortality, ill-health, and public health costs are presented to create a mass reaction, a group of people, in this case obese or fat people are then stigmatised, and consequently presented as a threat to the nation's social order and moral values. An alleged breach of the accepted limits of morality like this is usually at the centre of a moral panic, with the aim to create moral outrage towards a group of people or phenomenon. This then calls for increased social control over the alleged problem and an appeal to the authorities. Although the motivation behind moral panic might originally be benign, i.e., to improve the health of the population, it may often lead to further stigmatisation and marginalisation of the group it targets. This has certainly been the case with the panic surrounding the obesity "epidemic".

The obesity epidemic discourse has been emotive and moralising in tone, and it has frequently employed scare tactics and hyperbole as rhetorical devices (Harjunen 2004; LeBesco 2010). It would be justified to claim that the result was a full-blown moral panic over obesity in a number of countries, including the US, UK, and Finland (Boero 2012; Gard and Wright 2005; Harjunen 2004). Since this time the "obese" have been vilified, demonised and blamed for causing a wide array of problems.

Some of the headlines and stories about obesity on the BBC World website in 2007 and 2008, when the obesity epidemic discourse had reached one of its high-points, illustrate my claim. Obesity was called a contagious disease (26 July 2007);

a demolisher of the public health system (9 September 2007); and as not only a health risk but a pandemic (23 October 2007). In addition, child obesity was described as a form of child neglect (17 July 2007) which could lead to the child being taken away from the parents and into care (27 February 2007). But perhaps one of the most striking headlines of all was seen on 14 October 2007 when the problem of obesity was likened to climate change. In the spring of 2008, the BBC posed the question of how to defuse "the obesity time bomb" (7 March 2008), which was growing every day in the form of overweight children. In May 2008, the BBC World website even went so far as to inform its readers that "obesity" was responsible for many of the ills of the world including climate change, fuel prices, and world hunger (16 May 2008). In mid-August another headline claimed that obesity in the UK was "equal to a terror threat" (14 August 2008). All of these studies were also reported in Finland in a similar sensationalist vein. In fact, in Finland a headline in the military personnel's magazine hinted that fatness was also a threat to national security. In other words, overweight conscripts to the military were described as hampering Finland's military defence (Sivonen 2014).

It is telling that many of the above claims about fatness or about the issues caused by fatness, have a much wider context when we look more closely. It seems that many of the hot topics for a global neoliberal economy are bundled into the obesity epidemic discourse, such as the state of the environment, the welfare state, medicalisation, food politics, world politics, the morals of the nation, and the effects of neoliberal capitalism. The language of the headlines and the news stories emphasise the idea that fatness is out of control, it is spreading like wildfire, and that it will destroy not only societies or national economies, but the whole planet. In other words, "obesity" has been declared a danger that touches all levels of humanity socially, politically and economically; or at least it has been effectively constructed as such.

It seems that in the wake of the obesity epidemic discourse, fatness has become a symbolic or metaphorical illness in society over the last decade. By this I mean that the dominant obesity discourse not only frames fatness as a medical condition that affects the individual but also depicts the obese individual as the source of many social problems. Fatness has thus become a metaphor or symbol of those things detrimental to society.

Susan Sontag has written about cultural myths and metaphors concerning certain illnesses in two books: *Illness as Metaphor* (1978) and *Aids and Its Metaphors* (1989). She says that myths and metaphors used to discuss illnesses influence our understanding of the origins of illnesses, the personal characteristics of the patients, and their treatment in society. Sontag defines metaphors as "giving the thing a name that belongs to something else", and notes that they have been used throughout history to discuss the body, illness, and health. A view akin to Sontag's has been put forth by Barry Glassner (1999, pp. 151–179) who has observed that some illnesses in the history of medicine seem to have been interpreted as such "because they have been seen as indicative of some unresolved cultural and social conflicts". He calls these illnesses "metaphorical illnesses".

Sontag wrote specifically about metaphors associated with tuberculosis, cancer, and Aids as well as the use of these diseases themselves as metaphors. She links these diseases to certain historical periods in time, and claims that especially cancer and Aids have occupied a place as the most vilified diseases of the twentieth century. In the light of the obesity epidemic discourse, it is not so far-fetched to claim that it is now obesity that has, in many ways, taken over this role today.

Interestingly, among the metaphors Sontag mentions are those that depict illnesses as either some kind of "pollution", or in military terms. Both types of metaphor are frequently used in the obesity epidemic discourse. Talking about obesity metaphorically as this "epidemic" promotes the view that it is globally virulent, spreading uncontrollably, and threatening everyone – anyone can become fat if they are not careful. The obesity epidemic discourse thrives on the notion that there is a need to regain control of bodies that have been left uncontrolled for too long. Sontag (2002, pp. 133–134, 149) says that using metaphors which make something seem contagious when in reality it is not, may create a division between those who have the illness and those who do not. This encourages seeing the illness as a punishment for being a certain kind of person. Allusion to this contagion divides people into the normal "us", and the "others" who are not.

Military metaphors are also used to depict illnesses. It is common to talk about a "battle", "struggle", or "war against" some "danger", "threat", or "terror", which emphasises that the problem is being seriously dealt with, and requires aggressive treatment. These have all been used in connection to obesity too. For example, there is "the war on obesity"; people are encouraged to "battle the bulge"; dieting is talked about as a constant struggle of vigilance, and so on. As we have seen, news headlines have referred to obesity as a "terrorist threat", or as a "time-bomb" waiting to go off (see e.g. Biltekoff 2007; Herndon 2005; Kyrölä 2007). As Sontag (2002) points out, the use of military metaphors is harmful, because they increase the stigmatisation of the people seen to be suffering from these illnesses. There is certainly a difference between being at war against the disease and being at war against the people who have the disease, but the importance of making this distinction is often forgotten or just ignored. In short, military metaphors provide a target for public concern, but often it is simply the individuals or their behaviour which "take the flak", as it were. The obesity epidemic discourse has succeeded in evoking all of the metaphors above.

There is one specific type of metaphor that I have seen so far only used in connection with obesity. This metaphor connects fatness with public economy directly. While an individual's fatness is being discussed in economic terms as a "risk, surplus, excess, waste", it seems that the fat body has also come to metaphorically represent how neoliberal governments would like to portray a "bloated" public economy in need of trimming and cuts. Interventions that aim at changing the fat body are treated as analogous to interventions that are needed to fix the ailing public economy. The language of dieting has become part of economic rhetoric. For example, the Finnish Finance Minister, Jyrki Katainen noted in a speech in 2010 that "the public economy needs to go on a diet" (*YLE* 2010a). EU Commissioner Olli Rehn for his part stated that the "overgrown public sector needs to be slimmed down to a size that the economy can maintain" (Hölttä 2013), while citizens are encouraged to "tighten [their] belt[s]" (Elonin 2014), and negotiations concerning cuts to be made in the social and health sector are referred to in terms of training and exercise (Orjala 2015).

One possible reason why the fat body has come to represent the degeneration of our public economy, public healthcare, and our morals, among other things, is the rise of neoliberal rationality in society. I propose that fatness and the fat body have come to represent the contradictions of neoliberal times – they represent excess, surplus, and wastefulness, not just in bodies, but in society too. In a neoliberal culture which treats people as economic units, bodies as another kind of commodity, health as an expense, and being healthy as a chore, fatness is metonymically connected to everything that is detested in the neoliberal discourse. The obesity epidemic discourse and the moral panic surrounding it can be read as symptomatic of a more general anxiety over life in late capitalist society. When that worry is channelled into a group of people who are seen both as a symptom and as one source of the worry, a convenient scapegoat is acquired, which helps to camouflage the inequalities and injustices that are actually responsible for those anxieties.

Notes

1 Information on height and weight measurements has been collected for scientific and statistical use since the mid-nineteenth century (e.g. Oliver 2006). However, the possibility for individuals to know and monitor their body weight routinely as a part of everyday life is a fairly recent phenomenon. Only in the mid-nineteenth century, did the development of the spring scales, already invented in the eighteenth century, make it possible to measure body weight more accurately. Personal scales first started appear in private homes in the 1920s and 1930s.Perhaps coincidentally, the first attempts to treat fatness by weight loss also took place in the mid-nineteenth century, when the British medical doctor William Banting introduced the first weight-loss diet (Huff 2001, p. 39).
2 The case of female body size will be discussed specifically in Chapter 8.

4 The economisation of health and the fat body

Economy has permeated the discourses and practices of health to such an extent that it is justified to talk about "economisation of health". Health is increasingly understood and discussed in terms of the economy whether we are talking about its structural, institutional, cultural, or individual aspects. In welfare states, public healthcare systems are being downsized and reorganised in order to increase their productivity and cost-effectiveness while the private healthcare sector is growing. Health is a lucrative business, and we have gradually been moving away from talking about citizens who have a right to care and social security within a welfare state, towards talking about clients who are perceived as consumers of healthcare services. The ideal users of these services are self-managing individuals who are able to make rational choices concerning their own health and healthcare within the healthcare market. Health is thus increasingly seen in terms of investment and cost, and individuals are encouraged to approach it as a commodity that can be bought, sold, and invested in.

In this chapter, I will discuss the economisation of health and healthcare institutions particularly in the Finnish context. My aim is to illustrate the links between the economisation of healthcare, health, and the demonisation of fatness. I will first give a short overview of the development of health and social services as part of the public welfare state and then discuss their neoliberalisation and some central principles of neoliberal health policy in the context of Finland in the last few decades. This is followed by a discussion of health inequalities and the obesity epidemic in the light of two action plans drawn up by the National Institution for Health and Welfare (THL) in Finland, namely *The First Finnish National Action Plan to Reduce Health Inequalities 2008–2011* (2008) and *The National Obesity Programme 2012–2015: Overcoming Obesity – Well-being from Healthy Nutrition and Physical Activity* (Working Group for the National Obesity Programme 2013).

How has neoliberal governmentality (through the economisation of health services) contributed to the way fat bodies are seen as expensive or costly bodies? How does the emphasis put on health costs both literally as well as symbolically affect our understanding of health and healthy bodies?

Health and the public welfare state

Finland has a Nordic-style welfare state, the typical features of which are universal healthcare, a strong public sector, the equal treatment of citizens, small differences in income, and a relatively high level of social benefits. The historical development of the Finnish welfare state starts from the poor laws and poor relief of the nineteenth century (Satka 1995) but for the purposes of this book, I will concentrate on the period from the 1960s onwards. In this time the most rapid development of the welfare state took place (somewhat later than in other Nordic countries) and then it gradually began to be dismantled. The guidelines for this Finnish social policy were outlined in Pekka Kuusi's *Social policy for the 1960s* (1961),[1] in which he emphasised democracy, social equality, and economic growth as essential goals (Kettunen 2001, p. 231). One of the key differences between welfare state policy and the preceding poor laws has been its egalitarian nature. All citizens are covered by social security, not just the ones considered to be in greatest need. In Finland, similar to other Nordic countries, a citizen's social rights (following the notion of social citizenship by T.H. Marshall [1950]) are considered to be the cornerstone of equality, and that these social rights enable citizens to have the means to be both free and equal. In fact, this right to social security is written in the Constitution of Finland (731/1999).

The 1970s were a time when welfare state services and benefits in Finland grew rapidly (Kettunen 2001, p. 226) to the point at which, by the 1980s, the range and standard of services and benefits on offer were in many ways at their most extensive. However, criticism of the welfare state system had already begun long before it had reached this peak (Kettunen 2001, p. 231), and reorganisation and restructuring of the welfare state began gradually in the 1980s and accelerated in the 1990s (Eräsaari 2002; Yliaska 2014). Welfare-state academics generally agree that the neoliberal turn in Finland took place during the recession in the early and mid-1990s. While the welfare state reform of the 1990s may not have been caused by this recession, it certainly facilitated and accelerated it (Henriksson and Wrede 2008; Julkunen 2004). During and after the recession, the neoliberalisation of public policy including healthcare was promoted as a necessary rationalisation. Downsizing and cuts to public healthcare services were seen as inevitable in the context of economic recovery (Hirvonen 2014, p. 10). It was during this time that the so called "new public management" started to spread more rapidly to the public sector and privatisation, cost-efficiency, outsourcing, and cost-effectiveness became the latest buzzwords in economic discourse; and this started to have an effect in the field of social and health policy in Finland, where previously the market did not play such a significant role.

Welfare states were never simply built on pure altruism nor to just improve people's living conditions – macroeconomic concerns have always played a part too (Yliaska 2014). However, different welfare state models have taken different stances towards the market. The Nordic style of welfare state was built on the notion that an unregulated market can cause a great deal of damage, and so the state must offer its citizens social and economic protection from its fluctuations, for example, in the form of universal social and sickness insurance. Central to the Nordic model has been the notion that education, health, and social care are investments in a nation's long-term economic growth and prosperity. State-sponsored services and benefits secure the creation of a capable, healthy, and socially stable workforce. Welfare state policies such as universal healthcare have played a vital role in levelling social and health inequalities between socioeconomic groups (Palosuo *et al.* 2009).

The Finnish healthcare system has been largely publicly-funded, with a much smaller private healthcare sector. Municipalities are responsible for organising primary healthcare for their residents, with primary care provided in healthcare centres and secondary or tertiary care in regional hospitals (upon referral). Meanwhile the private healthcare sector, partially subsidised by the Social Insurance Institution (SII), has provided occupational healthcare and specialised medical care. Private healthcare providers, which range from companies to associations and foundations, can sell their services to municipalities, joint municipal authorities, and directly to individual clients.

So, although universal healthcare still applies in principle, the Finnish healthcare system is not exactly equal in practice. The structural organisation and division of healthcare into a two-tier system is partly to blame; and this has been acknowledged. For example, in 2010 a well-known professor of medicine, Matti Kekomäki, noted in an interview for *Suomen Kuvalehti* magazine that Finland is no longer a model country for healthcare, but "a model country for a care paradox" (Hynynen 2010). Those who can use occupational healthcare services, buy private health insurance, or have the financial means to purchase services from the private sector, have better access to healthcare in terms of waiting times and specialised medical care. As resources in public healthcare have diminished, those who have to rely on municipal healthcare (the unemployed, the poor, the aged) have to deal with, for example, queues of weeks or months to get any kind of specialised healthcare.

The problems in public healthcare have not gone unnoticed by healthcare corporations and they have actively expanded their operations to the field of primary care. Pressure to cut expenses, combined with recruitment problems especially in more remote areas, has led to the outsourcing of medical staff to healthcare centres. In the most extreme cases, municipalities have outsourced their entire healthcare service to companies that are owned by international corporations, in the hope of making savings. According to the Finnish Ministry of Social Affairs and Health (2015), the number of private social and health service providers has grown throughout the 2000s. Currently, the private sector provides a quarter of all services in the field (Ministry of Social Affairs and Health website 9 October 2015). There is now therefore a significant healthcare market in Finland.

Currently, there are major reforms to social and healthcare underway in Finland; since these are still very much in the planning stage, I will not go into them more deeply here. One of the changes to the present-day system we do know will happen is that, instead of being organised according to municipality, social and healthcare services will be organised according to autonomous areas specifically created for that purpose, and that these new authorities will be able to choose from a range of public, private, and third-sector service providers. At the very least, this will mean that the number of private businesses working in the public health sector will grow; this has been marketed to the electorate as meaning there will be a greater choice. The Ministry of Social Affairs and Health says on its website that the goal of these reforms is twofold: to diminish the inequalities in health and well-being, and to reduce the costs of the current health system.

Neoliberal healthcare

The economisation of healthcare is not a new phenomenon in countries such as the US where it has been a longstanding practice for people to buy private health insurance, and where one's personal resources have a direct effect on the quality, coverage, and availability of healthcare services. However, this has marked a sea change in a country like Finland. As Brown (2003, p. 3) notes, neoliberal economic policy favours the market and rejects state-sponsored welfare policies. In countries like Finland, where the public sector has been relatively large, adopting a neoliberal economic policy has meant strengthening the private sector at the expense of the public. Economic growth is the main priority of neoliberalism and everything else is subordinate to that goal. In neoliberal parlance, welfare state institutions are branded as inefficient, expensive, and spendthrift with taxpayers' money (e.g. World Bank 1993). This is somewhat ironic since private health corporations are often owned by multinationals and typically do not pay taxes in the countries where they operate, thus they do not help to alleviate the tax burden. The need to increase the efficiency of services (based on the rationale of "saving taxpayers money") is then used to justify downsizing public services. Then, when the downsized public institutions cannot answer quickly enough to the demand for services, the argument for transferring service provision to the market is given, when in fact the mandate for this already effectively took place when the downsizing occurred in the first place. Those who are then dissatisfied with the consequent reduction in capacity and quality of public services, and most crucially, who have the money to pay for it, can buy these services privately.

The neoliberal coup is complete when the state buys the same services from the private health market that it used to originally provide itself (and often for a lower price). The state then offers this service to the public in the name of increased consumer choice. So not only is the private market increasingly working alongside, but also within the public sector. In the process, as part of their marketing strategies, private companies have tailored their services to the prospective client pool, and in particular those who will have the financial means to afford them. It seems that the main problem for the neoliberal rationale behind all this is not so much the low cost-effectiveness or wastefulness of public services, as this has been shown to not always be the case; it is more the fact that if the public sector is the only provider of a service, it is construed as a threat to free competition in the marketplace – the basic premise of neoliberalism.

Alongside changing structures and institutions the role of the individual changes too: they are pushed towards taking more responsibility for their own health within these increasingly market-oriented structures and institutions. This means they are encouraged to act more as clients and consumers than as patients, and that responsibility for basic decisions concerning health and the funding of healthcare is increasingly placed on private individuals rather than the state. As Ventura notes, neoliberal culture encourages individuals to feel solely responsible for their lives and not entitled to assistance from the larger social structure (2012, p. 4). The economisation of health is thus a perfect example of how neoliberal governmentality drives individuals towards becoming self-reliant entrepreneurial subjects. Ventura goes on further to note that

> the omnipresence of market rationality [. . .] makes the ideology of consumer choice appear to be the essence of freedom and encourages us to see ourselves as atomized individuals who alone are the source of our successes or the blame for our failures – indeed, to define success and failure in market terms.
>
> (2012, p. 11)

This public–private divide in healthcare is clearly illustrated in the public discussion on fatness too. Fatness is seen as an expense and major burden on the public sector, while individuals are encouraged to think of weight-loss as a personal investment and of their bodies as a commodity. Indeed, talking about investment is not a mere figure of speech in this context. People spend billions of dollars in the US alone to buy products and services that promise weight-loss. According to Marketdata Enterprises (2014), a market research company that tracks the weight-loss industry in the US, Americans alone spent around 60 billion dollars on diet products and services in 2013. This figure included diet meals, drugs, and gym memberships among other things.

In the book, *The New Public Health: Discourses, Knowledges, Strategies*, Peterson and Lupton (1996) made an observation that health had begun to be discussed more and more in the context of the economy. They connected this tendency to the expansion of neoliberal governmentality that was taking place at around the same time. In Finland it took a while longer to notice the direction in which policymaking was heading. By the early 2000s the economisation and commercialisation of health services was already well underway in Finland, but still not easily identifiable. Finnish health communication scholars Aarva and Lääperi noted the changes in media discussions concerning health in Finland in their 2005 study. It looked into two major Finnish newspapers' health-related articles featuring in their editorial pages in 2002 and 2003. They found that arguments based on the premise of economics rather than well-being were increasingly being used to discuss health, as they complied with the "dominant societal atmosphere" of "financial growth, consumption, return, and investments" (2005, p. 75); but they made no attempt to analyse this "atmosphere" further. By describing it as an "atmosphere" in this context was unintentionally hiding and naturalising something that was not in reality a haphazard development, but a result of years of systematic policymaking, tightening resources and cutting back on healthcare budgets. It seems that already at this time neoliberal rationale was able to spread little by little, and step by step, to pertinent fields of society.

This kind of development has of course not been restricted to Finland; the neoliberal reform of health services has been consciously promoted by influential transnational organisations such as the World Bank. In 1993, the World Bank released a milestone report called *Investing in Health*, which provided an overview of recommended neoliberal policies in healthcare. The aim seemed to be to create healthcare systems that followed a neoliberal rationale around the world. The report aimed its message at a global audience and proposed a new approach for the finance and organisation of health services in both developed and developing countries (World Bank 1993).

In the report, existing health services were accused of misusing resources, unequal access, inefficiency, and growing costs. Neoliberal reforms were proposed because the overall quality of public health services was found to be inferior to healthcare providers in the private sector. The public sector was described as inefficient, their management systems too centralised, and their workers unmotivated. In comparison, private healthcare providers were described as efficient and providing better quality care (World Bank 1993). And yet, while some of these grounds might have been true, the report did not really take into account the variation between public healthcare systems around the world.

In the report, the need to improve the cost-effectiveness of healthcare was emphasised by, for example, proposing that the less cost-effective treatments be transferred to the private sector. It proposed that state-sponsored care be limited to only certain groups of people and certain kinds of illnesses. The introduction of user fees and the removal of legislative obstacles to private healthcare providers were also recommended, to encourage private health insurance, self-regulation, and financing. Competition between the public and private sectors in health was seen as a chance to improve care facilities; and so the government was advised to privatise and then outsource services. In some instances the report admitted that government regulation needed to remain in place to prevent an increase in health inequalities based purely on socioeconomic differences (World Bank 1993). In hindsight, it is quite remarkable how consistently the neoliberalisation of health services has followed the recommendations made in the report.

Health inequalities

The World Bank report discussed above is a clear indicator of the neoliberalisation of healthcare systems. It appears, for all intents and purposes, to be ideologically motivated and actively looking for the state to play a diminishing role as care provider; and first in the firing line were those national healthcare systems that were already well developed and providing universal healthcare.

Welfare states were built on the principles of egalitarianism. The goal was to give people equal opportunities in life whatever their social position and background, particularly in terms of education, healthcare, and social care. The effects of the global neoliberal economy have reached Finland though, as differences in income between socioeconomic groups have grown, the labour market has become increasingly unstable and fragmented, and the phenomenon of the working poor has emerged. In conjunction with this, the neoliberalisation of public policy – particularly health services – has contributed to differences in health between socioeconomic groups in Finland. In fact, after two decades of increasingly neoliberal policies, health inequality stemming from socioeconomic differences has returned (Palosuo *et al.* 2009).

According to researchers at the Finnish National Institute for Health and Welfare, health inequalities based on socioeconomic status have grown significantly over the past twenty years (Palosuo *et al.* 2009). Income differences have grown fast over the past two decades, and although the differences are smaller than for example in many other OECD countries, a simultaneous erosion of public and social policy has meant that there is now a growing number of people who experience long-term poverty and consequent social and health problems, such as food insecurity, in Finland. The recession in the early and mid-1990s is an important watershed in this respect. The unemployment rate rose rapidly, reaching 17 per cent at its peak, and has never dropped back to pre-recession levels, even during the economic boom of the early 2000s. In fact, that period of economic growth did not benefit everyone equally, and the proportion of people in low-income groups has risen consistently since the mid-1990s (Statistics Finland: income distribution statistics). In particular, the number of poor families rose during and after the recession (Palosuo *et al.* 2009, p. 13).

Alongside income differences, health inequalities between socioeconomic groups have grown during the past few decades (Palosuo *et al.* 2009, p. 11). The data that the research project on working poor in Finland collected, confirms the links between health and poverty. People who wrote about their experiences frequently talked about the effects of a poor financial situation on their health, their food choices, and ultimately their body. Some could not even afford to see a doctor in a municipal healthcare centre due to the initial fee that is charged (which varies by municipality); others could not purchase medication that had been prescribed for them; and others said that they did not have money to buy enough food, had sometimes gone without, had to rely on food banks for basic sustenance, or to eat left-over food from grocery shops, supermarkets, and restaurants. Many recounted different types of bodily effects from poverty of which weight gain was one. The inability to buy and eat healthy food was mentioned as a direct result of poverty as well as the inability to find time for exercise due to exhaustion or lack of time. As one of the informants aptly wrote: "poverty goes into your body".

Today there are therefore significant differences in health and life expectancy between educational and socioeconomic groups in Finland. Those in higher social groups and with a higher education live longer and are healthier. The data from 1990 shows that 25-year-olds who had tertiary level education expected to have on average thirteen more healthy years than those with only a basic education. Long-term morbidity is reported to be 50 per cent more prevalent in the lowest educational and social groups, when compared to the highest groups. Socioeconomic status has an effect on well-being, health, life expectancy and the use of health services. Half of the differences in mortality between socio-economic groups are caused by differences in alcohol use and smoking, both of which are more prevalent in lower socioeconomic groups. Meanwhile, if life expectancy is examined in the light of income differences, this inequality is even more pronounced. From 1988 to 2007, the gap between the highest and the lowest quintiles has widened by 5.1 years among men, and 2.9 years among women. Socioeconomic differences thus affect life expectancy significantly (Tarkiainen *et al.* 2011).

Remarkably, health inequalities had already been growing for well over a decade in Finland, before this was properly acknowledged by the health authorities. According to Palosuo *et al.* (2009), even health policy professionals failed to recognise that socioeconomic health inequality was growing. One explanation for this oversight is that there was a greater emphasis on studying regional and gender health differences in health policy measures at this time, which means there was a lack of appropriate data. Other possible reasons that have been cited are that the topic was considered politically difficult, and there was not sufficient academic interest in investigating rising health inequalities.

The first Finnish *National Action Plan to Reduce Health Inequalities* was not published until 2008. In the report it was stated that social factors needed to be addressed to erase health inequalities and this needed to be ongoing and not limited to the field of health policy. In a way the report seemed to return to the original motivation behind creating an extensive welfare state – i.e. to maintain a sizeable and qualified workforce and economic prosperity in the nation. However, there was also what might be called a neoliberal spin on all of this, in that the arguments for diminishing or erasing health inequalities were above all economic, and with an emphasis on work. In the same plan (National Institute for Health and Welfare 2008, p. 71), it was clearly noted that promoting employees' health was in the interest of all those in the labour market, as competent and healthy workers were more productive and would stay in the workforce for longer. The health of employees directly equated with a nation's competitiveness, and in this way Finland's success in the global market would be every citizen's responsibility.

> Promoting working ability and health and reducing health inequalities is in the interests of both the employers' and employees' organisations and their members. A healthy employee is a major competitive and productive factor for the employer. Concern for staff well-being and health will be an important advantage in the future when employers compete for skilled and competent workers, especially if the predicted labour shortage becomes a reality. As the labour force ages and age groups moving into working life grow smaller, everyone must do their best to further the competitive ability of Finland on the global market.
>
> (National Institute for Health and Welfare 2008, p. 71)

The good health of the population is a central part of the human capital that is an increasingly important prerequisite for a sound national economy and industrial competitiveness. People put a high value on their health, which also influences their choices as consumers of goods and services. The demand for healthy and health-promoting products and well-being services is growing rapidly. Thus, health is important for our economy in many ways. Economic activities are a major part of the everyday environment that is central to our health. They manifest themselves as working environments, as environmental impacts of the industrial plants and production, as products and services, and as the impact of marketing on the informational and cultural environment. In terms of implementation of this National Action Plan, it is crucial that companies see their potential and their obligation to promote health in cooperation with other parties with similar interests.

(National Institute for Health and
Welfare 2008, p. 72)

From both microeconomic and macroeconomic perspectives, it is clear that health is of instrumental importance. After all, in economic discourse, an individual-trial competitiveness. People put a high value on their'rom both microeconomic and macroeconomic perspectives, it is clear that health is of instrumental importanowth is becoming more prevalent and is increasingly apparent in public health promotions and the growing popularity of workplace wellness programmes. These have also been criticised, among other things, for establishing weight limits and other conditions on promotions or a rise in salary (e.g. Cederströe and Spicer 2015; Kirkland 2014).

In the report, an effort is made to engage a wide variety of actors to reduce health inequalities. This includes doctors, schools, employers, and companies, but ultimately the final responsibility is being laid at the feet of the individual. Tellingly, in this plan, the relationship between health and the economy is extended to cover people's consumption of health products and services, as well as environmental health. What we eat or where we live, for example, are both clearly class-bound issues, and the ability to make healthy choices is partly an issue of class privilege, which is not fully recognised in the report.

Health as an issue in its many manifestations is presented as inevitably interconnected with the economy. Health is thus seen not just as a value and goal in itself. From the business point of view, health-consciousness is also a profit-generating phenomenon and it is this which enables health to be seen as yet another commodity, and for people who consume health products and services to be seen as yet another market. I argue that this emphasis on every citizen's responsibility to ensure their productivity and profitability by working to be as healthy as possible is a perfect example of neoliberal governmentality in action, which is also reflected in the obesity epidemic discourse (OED).

The obesity epidemic discourse as a form of neoliberal governmentality

As the obesity epidemic discourse progressed and spread throughout the early 2000s, fatness became the target of an ever-increasing set of activities that were designed to solve the "epidemic". Countless action programmes, national obesity plans, and campaigns have been initiated in the fight against it all around the world. Some of the activities were sponsored by public health bodies with the lowering of public health expenditure (and overall well-being of the population) in mind, but those who have benefited the most from the obesity epidemic discourse have been the enterprises that comprise the diet industry (e.g. Cheek 2008; Harrison 2012; LeBesco 2011).

The obesity epidemic discourse has not only helped justify policies, sanctions, and action programmes concerning the prevention and treatment of fatness within the public health sector but has also created a great deal of business opportunities for those who stand to benefit from the medicalisation and stigmatisation of fatness. The obesity epidemic discourse can be held as a model example of an issue in which the interests of the public and private sector are mutual, but their gains lie in opposite directions. The public health sector aims to diminish the obesity rate to cut public health expenses, while the private sector produces different types of health products and services and ultimately aims to make a profit from it. For this to happen, it is obviously more beneficial for the problem to persist and thereby generate more revenue (Cheek 2008; Harrison 2012). So while the public health sector obviously has a genuine interest in improving people's health and preventing disease both economically and ethically, it has also quite possibly been exacerbating the issue – by cutting its budget and outsourcing certain services to the private sector.

Fittingly, the obesity epidemic discourse has brought medical experts and businesses to the same table in the name of preventing obesity. Finland's first national obesity programme was a result of such cooperation. The programme was titled, *The National Obesity Programme 2012–2015: Overcoming Obesity – Well-being from Healthy Nutrition and Physical Activity*. The programme was published in 2013 and work was coordinated by the National Institute for Health and Welfare (THL). The programme was designed to address obesity as a public health problem, and encourage different actors in society to join forces to prevent and reduce obesity. Its main goal was to "improve the health and welfare of the population and to maintain its ability to work and function" (Working Group for the National Obesity Programme 2013, p. 12). A wide range of actors and partners participated in this programme, including municipalities, health services, schools, early years' settings, the defence forces, public health organisations, sports organisations, trade unions, employers, the food industry, trade unions, catering service providers, research institutes, and the media.

Implementation of the programme was planned so that the different collaborating parties would incorporate the programme's goals into their own activities and environment. Meanwhile, the THL would report on the measures implemented, offer information, collaborate with the various actors, and track the progress and outcomes of the programme via research and health monitoring.[2] In the first pages of the programme the cause of obesity is explained in biomedical terms.

> Weight gain is a result of a long-term imbalance in consumption of energy. Other factors that contribute to weight are technologization of society and a number of economic, cultural, social, and psychological factors. Healthy diet and exercise are the primary means to prevent weight gain.
>
> (2013, p.13)

Because of this biomedical understanding of fatness, the programme mostly concentrates on nutrition and exercise, and the conditions and contexts that might in fact have something to do with what people eat and how they exercise are not discussed at any length. This is typical of medicalisation and characteristic of most health promotion (Broom 2008). Although it is recognised in passing that there are structural problems, which cannot be solved purely by health promotion or medical intervention, there are very few concrete suggestions in the programme as to how problems, such as a lack of funds to buy healthy food, or lack of time to prepare it, might be solved. This leaves the main responsibility for weight management on the shoulders of the individual, and makes the goal to give "everyone the possibility to make healthy food choices" sound quite hollow, especially considering that the very same institution was also responsible for the *National Action Plan to Reduce Health Inequalities*.

The starting premise of the programme, which traces the cause of rising obesity to a "higher standard of living and changes in lifestyles and the living environment" immediately raises some questions. Although it might seem accurate in the light of Finland during the course of the twentieth century, it seems less accurate in the first decades of the twenty-first, during which time income differences and health inequalities have grown and the Finnish population has become increasingly socially segregated. This is the first indication that the correspondence between certain structural issues, such as poverty and the economy, and the prevalence of fatness have not been given due consideration. It is now commonly accepted that being overweight and obese is more common in lower socioeconomic groups, and that health inequalities have increased in Finland over the course of the 2000s (e.g. Erola 2009). Those who are wealthy and privileged tend to be thinner than those who are not. Fatness is associated with low income and limited means rather than a higher standard of living. In the *National Obesity Programme* it is noted that the children of parents with a higher educational background are on average thinner than those of parents with less education (see, e.g. Berg 2010), but otherwise there is little analysis of the correlation between socioeconomic position and weight. This seems a crucial omission if this programme is compared to the reports on rising health inequalities in Finland made by the same institution at around the same time. Socioeconomic differences are mentioned in passing, but they are not taken as a basis for planning in the *National Obesity Programme*.

It would clearly be better that fatness be approached from a wider perspective than simply that of biomedicine, and for socioeconomic and environmental issues to be taken into account. However, the primary interest of a business is ultimately the profit it makes, not the weight or health of the consumer, and not overall public health, especially if maintaining the problem is in their own business interest. This was exemplified in the case of an excise tax on sweets, ice cream and soft drinks that was introduced in Finland at the beginning of 2011. Public health concerns and the obesity epidemic discourse were partly behind the introduction of the tax, and yet, as soon as certain energy-rich products were taxed more heavily, new increasingly snack-like versions of products such as biscuits and health bars (which remained exempt from the tax) began to flood the market. Although consumption of sugary products that were covered by this tax went down for a while, they began to rise again and eventually, after complaints from manufacturers and a decision by the EU Commission that collection of tax in this form was distorting competition between similar products, the tax will cease to be enforced at the end of 2016.

Some critics of the obesity epidemic discourse such as Markula (2008) are firmly of the opinion that the foundation of the obesity epidemic was and always has been economic. Guthman and DuPuis (2006, p. 429) for their part, have put forth the thesis that "neoliberalism both produces obesity and produces it as a problem". They claim that obesity as a problem is not external but internal to the logic of neoliberalism. If the neoliberal solution is, as Guthman and DuPuis (2006, p. 441) say, "commodification of everything", then both the problem of obesity and its solutions are part of the same broader issue. Guthman and DuPuis summarise that the "global–political economic contradictions of the neoliberal era are embodied" (2006, p. 429) and that this embodiment is in the fat body. In this work Guthman and DuPuis (2006, pp. 427–428) are discussing the politics of the obesity epidemic discourse in North America through the lens of neoliberalism as a political–cultural project, and as a form of governmentality. They point out how the demands of the neoliberal era from the point of view of the individual are essentially paradoxical. At the same time as these demands emphasise the benefits of freedom of choice and unbridled consumerism, they are stressing the importance of vigilant self-regulation:

> Neoliberal governmentality produces contradictory impulses such that the neoliberal subject is emotionally compelled to participate in society as both out-of-control consumer and self-controlled subject. [. . .] Those who can achieve thinness amidst this plenty are imbued with the rationality and self-discipline that those who are fat must logically lack; they then become the deserving in a political economy all too geared toward legitimizing such distinctions.
>
> (2006, p. 444)

This neoliberal economic logic would see people consuming constantly and as much as possible (as greater consumption will increase profit and overall economic growth). Everything can be bought from the market, be it items to do with eating, nutrition, health, or fitness. But at the same time the consumer is supposed to turn into an "entrepreneur" of one's own life, who is responsible, self-reliant, and invested in self-control (particularly of the body). The neoliberal body is thus encouraged to both consume and discipline itself at the same time, with further consumption being paradoxically encouraged to facilitate this disciplining process (in the form of dieting products etc.).

In the neoliberal economy, healthcare, social care, education, welfare (and in fact everything) can and should be made into commodities that can be marketed, bought, or sold (Guthman and DuPuis 2006). Eliminating or curing fatness might mean a healthier population in the long-run (not to mention smaller costs for the state and ultimately the taxpayer); but it is not always in the interest of neoliberal healthcare and all the industries that thrive off it. These industries include the pharmaceutical or diet industries, private clinics that offer bariatric surgery, and commercial health insurers. Ultimately, the neoliberal economy wants to increase health-related consumption, as the role of the citizen has been transformed into one of a consumer or entrepreneur. Consumption and one's role as a consumer is increasingly underlined even in the relationship between the citizen and the state. One becomes part of society first and foremost by being a good consumer and adopting an entrepreneurial approach to work, relationships, and the body, and one's value to society increasingly depends on an individual's ability to produce and consume. If individuals are not capable of being productive enough (in market terms), or performing consistently as a consumer, their limited value and role in society is somehow justified.

Harrison (2012, p. 331) claims that the diet industry turns "bodies into economic units from which profits can be reaped, despite its persistent failure to change bodies in the ways promised". It is obvious that maintaining the problem status of fatness benefits many a commercial actor. The obesity epidemic discourse has helped turn fatness into a lucrative business opportunity for the dietary, pharmaceutical, fitness, biotechnology, food, news, and entertainment industries among others. The dietary industry is particularly pertinent in that it needs returning customers that are unhappy with their weight, and people do return in spite of the fact mentioned earlier that the failure rate of diets is around 95 per cent (Aphramor and Gingras 2008). This means that only around 5 per cent of those who diet can keep the weight off permanently, or for more than a few years. In fact, these success and failure rates have remained surprisingly consistent over the years (e.g. Sarlio-Lähteenkorva 1999). The weight management industry is emblematic of some of the contradictions inherent in the present-day neoliberal health and body culture that is economised and commercialised. It tries to convince us that it is possible to both stay healthy – shorthand for thin – and thus fulfil the moral imperative of control and to continue to consume, if not food, then supplements, meal replacement products among others.

Labelling fatness as categorically unhealthy and as a disease (medicalisation), normalising the thin body, increasing the social pressure to be thin, and stigmatising fatness means the dietary industry creates a lot of consumers. Since there is as yet no effective, safe or indeed permanent ways to lose weight and remain thin, the market stays very lucrative. Stigmatising fatness and fat bodies only adds to the commercial demand of any products that promise relief from this stigma. The neoliberal economy wants this increased consumption anyway, and in the current fat-phobic environment, the fear of fatness provides a powerful drive to consume. In a sense, engaging in the possibly never-ending project of weight loss makes fat people the best consumers. And besides, the fat "customer", who can equally be anyone who just believes they are fat, or who is just afraid of becoming fat, is a returning customer.

Deservingness, morals, costs and investment

As discussed above, in a society that is organised according to neoliberal principles, individuals need to adopt the logic of the market when they think about their health. Health is a value in itself, but it is also valuable in other ways. Health increases the value of the body, which in itself is a product that can be created, sold, and optimised (c.f. Ventura 2012). In neoliberal culture, health is therefore more than just about being healthy, it is considered to be an integral part of a highly performing individual. A healthy body is a condition for optimal productivity and cost-effectiveness. Certain bodies (if they are unhealthy, fat, aged, depressed, or disabled) prevent a person from achieving the optimal results that neoliberal citizenship requires, for example staying in the workforce for as long as possible, working as effectively (and as much) as possible, staying healthy through vigorous exercise and eating nutritiously, and needing as little social or publicly funded assistance as possible.

In the age of neoliberalism, biopolitical control is (always) economic control too. The principles of neoliberal governmentality, i.e. market orientation and an entrepreneurial approach towards self-management, have become discursively transferred onto the notions of health and body. In effect, the value of an individual is based on an analysis of cost in which the logic of reverse thinking applies. The body is expected to be productive, cost-effective, and dynamic. The less the individual needs public services the more cost-effective and productive/profitable the individual appears from the state's point of view. However, the goal of neoliberal governmentality is not an individual who does not need or use any healthcare services, as that would lead to significant loss of power over the biopolitical regulation of the bodies. The ideal goal is to create individuals who take responsibility over their health to such a point that they no longer feel the state has a duty to care for them. In this way, the entrepreneurial subject of neoliberal governmentality feels a moral obligation to manage one's own health.

Wendy Brown has said that neoliberalism removes the barrier between morals and economics and creates a world wherein moral decisions are made through a cost–benefit analysis of what will affect the self. She says:

> in making the subject fully responsible for her or himself, neoliberalism equates moral responsibility with rational action; it erases the discrepancy

between economic and moral behavior by configuring morality entirely as a matter of rational deliberation about costs, benefits and consequences.

(2003, p. 6)

This relationship between economics and morals is clearly visible in the discussion concerning fatness, health and the economy. Bodies are evaluated as "good" or "bad" based on their apparent value (productivity) and/or their cost to society, which is based on their assumed health. Those bodies that are perceived as unhealthy are viewed as unproductive, expensive, and a burden to society, for their assumed costs to public healthcare. When people are categorised as expensive based on their personal characteristics, we are in effect evaluating people's social acceptability citizenship status according to their cost to society.

The dominance of this neoliberal rationale in the political, social, and medical contexts has also meant an increasing division of people into those who are seen to deserve care, benefits, and respectful treatment and those who are not. In a neoliberal society, people have to fulfil certain requirements to be eligible for services that were previously available to all, and this "prioritisation" is key to neoliberal practices. For example, whenever there is talk about a need to "prioritise" healthcare services, fat people are among the first that are singled out as not meeting certain criteria before they can be accepted as patients. Currently, patients are denied certain procedures (i.e. IVF, knee surgery) unless they have lost weight first. At regular intervals, it is proposed that fat people should start paying for their own healthcare or, at least, pay more for it (Hukkanen 2005). The reasoning behind this is that fat people are choosing to be fat and are thus choosing to be unhealthy. Fatness is seen as a self-inflicted and a sign of a failure to behave like a responsible healthy citizen. The moral responsibility is firmly placed on the shoulders of the individual.

According to neoliberal rationale, state-sponsored healthcare depends on patients' morals, insofar as it matters how they got the ailment in the first place. Those who become labelled as having "expensive" bodies are readily seen as neglecting to take personal responsibility of their bodies. Those who are assumed or appear to be irresponsible in this way are then seen as undeserving of state-sponsored services and are labelled as having costly bodies. In this kind of monetary and moral evaluation of cost effectiveness, those bodies that are already stigmatised or considered immoral are set to fail. The danger with this line of thought is that the fat body's assumed costliness has then been used extensively to monger fear and resentment, and to make moral judgments of fat bodies. It has also become one of the main arguments for the need to treat the fat body as unwell.

One's worthiness can be proven by morally virtuous behaviour. Those individuals or groups of people who are believed (or assumed) to take risks "willingly" or are seen as somehow "choosing" to make themselves ill by their irresponsible behaviour, do not get much sympathy. In the least, they should bear responsibility, financial or otherwise, for their alleged bad choices. This kind of moral evaluation of which people deserve the privilege of public services or benefits is a common notion. It is often heard in discussions concerning welfare benefits that individual citizens owe it to society to behave in a certain way in exchange for the "free" public social or healthcare they receive.

In a sense, individuals need to prove how they deserve the investment that society is making in them. Their responsibility to be healthy is thus to the whole of society. People who are in need of public services, particularly social services, are often blamed for creating their own predicament by somehow choosing to behave irresponsibly as if it was a moral question. Holding recipients of public healthcare services accountable for their choices is paradoxical when at the same time the scope of public healthcare services is diminishing (due to neoliberal restructuring, prioritising, and privatisation) and individuals' economic burden and responsibility over healthcare expenses are growing (Ayo 2012, p. 100).

Harrison (2012) has written that in neoliberal culture everyone is an economic unit. Health has turned into a merit and a sign of moral and fiscal solvency. Responsibility is evaluated, not only as certain type of behaviour in moral terms, but also by one's estimated costliness to society. Harrison (2012, p. 321) notes that this construct of fat bodies as costly allows for corporations and governments to "exploit some for the enrichment of others while reaping economic benefit from activities that harm human health to do so in relative impunity".

The need to battle the obesity epidemic is justified with the alleged financial cost that fat people cause in the form of public health expenses. Fatness features in neoliberal economics, not only via public sector healthcare expenses, however, but also via the consumption of a wide variety of commercial products and services. The catch in neoliberal healthcare is that whereas public spending on the care of individuals is calculated in terms of cost, their own spending on care and health is seen as an investment. The amount of money fat people spend in order to lose weight is one example of this kind of investment that individuals are supposed to make out of their own pocket.

Costliness and cost-effectiveness readily become moral terms when talked about in the neoliberal context of using public funds. Costing money to the state and "making other people pay for your allegedly bad choices" through taxation becomes a moral question. Consumption is the key here and the fact that health has become about consumption. When people buy health foods, diet supplements, diet meals, fitness, and health services from the private market, they are good consumers who *invest* in their own health. This is one of the paradoxes of the neoliberal logics when applied to bodies and health; there is a pressure that one appears to be in control and responsible, yet at the same time one should continue to consume as much as possible (Guthman and DuPuis 2006, p. 445). The very same fat bodies that are labelled as immoral and costly in the public sector somehow become very profitable and perhaps even moral (for generating revenue in the market) when they relocate to the private sector as consumers. In a sense, the ideal neoliberal body and health subject is thus not so much the person that abstains from using health services, but one that "consumes" (and therefore pays for) as many health services as possible and for as long as possible. In the end, it seems that, paradoxically, fatness is in demand in the neoliberal market place.

Not only does it provide an easy target and scapegoat for health cuts in the public sector, but also economic opportunities in the private. Guthman and DuPuis's (2006) claim that the neoliberal economy both creates fatness while at the same time condemning it seems to ring true here.

Notes

1 Original title: 60-luvun sosiaalipolitiikka.
2 As I am writing this, results of the programme have not yet been evaluated publicly and how well the implementation has succeeded is still unclear. My personal impression is that its profile has not been particularly high, then again, the idea of the programme was perhaps to cast as wide a net as possible rather than aim for maximum visibility.

5 Healthism and individual responsibility

In this chapter, I will examine health in more depth, and specifically from the perspective of an ideology and phenomenon of "healthism" – which draws profusely from a neoliberal rationale (Crawford 2006). Healthism makes health a matter of personal responsibility and free choice, and often a question of morals. The notion of health and healthy bodies that is promoted by healthism is not only exclusive, it also serves a specific function in neoliberal culture, and is thus a part of the neoliberal governmentality that produces certain type of bodies and subjects. Indeed, health is one of the principal arenas in which people are being moulded into neoliberal subjects. I will therefore discuss here the links between healthism and neoliberal governmentality and show how their joint effects reinforce the idea that fatness be understood as an individual's responsibility and enforce the fat stigma, and the phenomenon of "wellness" as a gendered mode of neoliberal healthism and its effects.

The ubiquity of healthism and its moral implications

In the last few decades, health has become an all-pervasive preoccupation in the west (Ayo 2012; Cheek 2008; Crawford 1980; 2006). Julianne Cheek (2008, p. 974), for example, has written that health is now almost "sacred" and that it has become not only a contemporary form of "the eternal quest for immortality", but also "a badge of honor by which we can claim to be responsible and worthy both as citizens and individuals". Meanwhile, Ayo (2012, p. 100) has observed that health consciousness is deeply embedded within the social fabric in the twenty-first century, and Crawford (2006, p. 404) for his part, notes that health has become an "increasingly unavoidable" and "continuous presence" in our lives, which demands a great deal of attention and resources. He says:

> The pursuit of health, in short, has become one of the more salient practices of contemporary life, commanding enormous social resources, infusing every major institutional field and generating an expansive professionalization and commercialisation, along with attendant goods, services and knowledge.
>
> (Crawford 2006, p. 404)

Interest in health, fitness, nutrition and overall well-being is undeniably high today (e.g. Ayo 2012; Cheek 2008; Crawford 2006). Many people seem to run marathons nowadays, or go to the gym, train for triathlons, go on trekking trips, meditate, do yoga, or practice mindfulness of some form or another. People's diets seem to have become increasingly diverse, yet at the same time very specific; many eliminate animal protein in their diets and follow vegetarian or vegan diets, but many are also sugar-free, wheat-free, gluten-free, dairy-free, carbohydrate-free, or all of the above. Some eat mainly proteins and fats, others favour carbohydrates, and some like their food unprocessed and uncooked. Fundamental aspects of life such as nutrition, physical exercise, and relaxation have thus become very complex and time-consuming endeavours that require a great deal of knowledge, funds, and technology, among other things.

Following these specific diets and fitness regimes often necessitates close monitoring of the body, its vital statistics, functions, and performance. Technologies that were previously used in mostly medical settings are now commonplace in our homes and on our bodies. Blood-pressure monitors have become a common household item, genetic testing kits can be ordered online for use at home, and various other new devices that give us information about our bodies come onto the market all the time. There are also numerous smart phone applications and plenty of other wearable technologies that help people to keep track of their caloric intake, heart rate, level of physical activity, quality of sleep, and so on, with the result that it is now possible to carry out quite sophisticated and comprehensive self-monitoring.

At the same time, health knowledge is now available on the internet from a wider variety of sources than ever (Crawford 2006, p. 415). Traditional authorities of health promotion such as the National Institute of Health and Social Affairs (THL) in Finland now have to compete with many other online sites and forums for credibility. The expertise of public health officials is thus often challenged by a new kind of market-oriented health expert – often self-made – which means that, more than ever, health is constantly debated in a wide variety of arenas from health policymaking and health promotion to popular media and culture. With a more and more extensively established internet, new studies and research results on health and fitness are reported daily, with an abundance of media devoted, for example, to health, fitness, training, nutrition, alternative modes of healthcare, and dieting.

In addition, the pursuit of health, especially through dieting and weight loss, has become a popular form of television entertainment. The obesity epidemic discourse has given life to whole new genres of popular culture, such as television shows devoted to competitive weight loss like *The Biggest Loser* or *You Are What You Eat*. Both of these shows have had localised versions of them made in many countries, among them Finland. Another genre that has clearly taken advantage of the obesity panic is the type of sensationalist and exploitative documentary that depicts the lives of and dramatic attempts by fat people to lose weight; these often use such monikers as the world's fattest man or woman, or the fattest city, state or country, and so on.

What I have described above is a culture that is imbued by "healthism", a phenomenon that was first named and identified by political economist Robert Crawford in his often cited 1980 article "Healthism and the Medicalization of Everyday Life". In a nutshell, healthism means that health is understood as the primary basic constituent of an individual's life and thus the priority in all one's efforts. Everything done, and every choice made, is evaluated through the lens of its effect (whether real or assumed) on the individual's health. It could be said that in a culture that is permeated by healthism, health is not something one automatically "has" any longer; it has to be earned through a continuous personal project requiring systematic work and strong commitment (c.f. Shilling 1993). Health has become constant "doing" by all possible means and people must be conscious of their health in all their choices and activities, for as Cheek notes, "being healthy does not mean not being ill" (Cheek 2008, p. 974), pointing out that we are always at risk of falling ill, as this can happen to any of us at any time.

The most notable features of healthism focus on the individual, personal responsibility, and the idea of free choice. In the context of healthism, health is understood in individualistic terms. It is understood as a matter of will which can be controlled by one's own actions, and yet somewhat paradoxically, "doing" of health is not volitional: Lupton (1995) has suggested that there is an "imperative of health" that prevails. In this respect, health is regarded as a duty; people are expected to pay attention to their health and monitor it themselves at all times. This "doing health" has become an essential part of managing the self and governing the body.

Healthism is a part of the medicalisation of society, which helps to define a range of issues in medical terms (e.g. Conrad 2007). One consequence is that health, having been transformed into a moral duty, is considered as the sum of an individual's own "good" choices (Harjunen 2009, p. 25), and illness is seen, in many ways, as the result of "bad" choices. Health thus becomes a question of personal success or failure in making those choices, and blame is apportioned accordingly, as the obesity epidemic discourse has amply shown. For instance, Cheek (2008, p. 981) has noted that in the era of biomedicalisation, "people are blamed for both their acts and their omissions – what they do wrong and what they fail to do right". In this context, controlling or appearing to control one's health has become a sign of being a responsible individual. The assumption is that if one "does health" the right way, it results in a body that will look "healthy". This healthy-looking body is a very normative construct though; its size, shape and style are clearly determined, as already discussed in Chapter 3. It is unfortunately very common to make assumptions about people's health based on their appearance. This is especially true regarding bodies that do not seem conform to this norm (medical or otherwise) of the healthy-looking body. The fat body is a particularly good example of this. Although it is not possible to know that much about a person's level of health and fitness based simply on the way they look, fat people are often automatically deemed unhealthy because of their size (Harjunen 2004a). This is one way in which the medicalisation of fat bodies has been very effective. It is habitually assumed that fat people are careless about their health, or at least are not doing it in a proper way since, if they were, they would not be fat, would they?

In healthist thinking, the work that is presumed to have been put into the body (judging from its appearance) is seen as an expression of an individual's inner life and character. Because of this, it is important to be able to produce a close facsimile of what is considered the visual approximation of a normative healthy body. The body thus becomes a manifestation of all the assumed effort put into its apparent health, whether this is actually true or not. It is evident that this health-ist conception of the morally virtuous and healthy body is normative and highly exclusive. First, only certain types of bodies are acceptable as healthy, and sec-ond, only certain types of subjects have the means to achieve this. Third, body size is obviously not the only difference that organises understanding of health and the healthy body. Health and what is considered a normative embodiment of health is for example gendered, classed, and racialised (Broom 2008, p. 132). The norms for a healthy body are different for women and men: in the case of women, as Dworkin and Wachs (2009) observed in their analysis of women's health and fitness magazines, health and fitness is often used as a means to express nor-mative feminine beauty and body ideals, rather than physical fitness, endurance, and strength *per se*. This normative understanding of femininity, for its part, draws from middle-class aesthetics and values (Skeggs 1997; 2005), as the white middle-class female body is considered to represent the "normal" body that other bodies are compared to and what they should strive to be like.

A distinct ideological kinship between healthism and neoliberalism has been detected by a number of academics (e.g. Ayo 2012, p. 100; Cheek 2008, p. 974; Crawford 2006). Cheek, for example, observes that current health and healthcare discourses have been shaped by liberal capitalism; while Ayo (2012, p. 100) states that health promotion "both reflects and reinforces the prevailing political ideol-ogy of neoliberalism and furthermore operates in such a way as to facilitate the making of the "good" and "healthy" citizen".

The emphasis that healthism puts on individual responsibility and choice clearly connects it to neoliberal rationale (Crawford 2006; Guthman and DuPuis 2006). The demand to relentlessly "do health" would seem to fit particularly well with a neoliberal rationale in which the body is a target of intense self-discipline and self-governance and its value is measured by its effectiveness and productiv-ity; and in this respect, it could be understood as one vehicle that carries neoliberal rationale into the body. Via healthist thought, and the demands it puts on the body, behaviour, and morals of the individual, neoliberal ideas can be transferred to the everyday personal management of the body. Healthism has been discussed spe-cifically as a form of governmentality that draws from capitalism and relies on the responsibilisation of people rather than direct coercion (Rose 1999).

As a discourse, healthism emerged in the late 1970s and early 1980s, at around the same time as neoliberalism started to spread in the US and in the UK (Crawford 2006; Harvey 2007). Crawford (2006, p. 410) has suggested that the importance of individual responsibility for one's health has had a significant role "in establishing the 'common sense' of neoliberalism's essential tenets".

He suggests that rising health consciousness in the 1970s in the USA helped to create "the ideology of personal responsibility" that was essential for the rise and success of neoliberal rationality. According to Crawford (2006, pp. 408–409), the notion of personal responsibility in health helped replace a more collectively minded understanding of economic and social well-being with neoliberal thought. There are thus fair grounds for me to argue that these joint effects of healthist and neoliberal thought have well and truly interlocked to manifest themselves, not only in the widespread economisation and commercialisation of health services but also in the way individuals "do health", and thus ultimately present in the bodies of individuals. By adopting the principles of healthism into our lives, we become part of its ideological apparatus and are more easily governed.

Healthist thinking prescribes that health is achieved as a result of an individual's own choices concerning lifestyle, behaviour, and attitudes; indeed, any perceived success or failure, for that matter, is an individual's own responsibility. In this way it comes remarkably close to the neoliberal idea of a self-reliant and self-governing individual. Healthist thought tends to overlook structural issues that affect health and the individual's ability to make decisions about it. Also the effects of different forms of inequality, such as sexism, racism, classism, ableism, and their intersectional effects are not taken into account. Crawford summarises the effects of healthism quite succinctly:

> Healthism situates the problem of health and disease at the level of the individual. Solutions are formulated at that level as well. To the extent that healthism shapes popular beliefs, we will continue to have a non-political, and therefore, ultimately ineffective conception and strategy of health promotion. Further, by elevating health to a super value, a metaphor for all that is good in life, healthism reinforces the privatization of the struggle for generalized well-being.
>
> (Crawford 1980, p. 366)

This tendency to focus on the individual is reflected in public health promotion that evokes a neoliberal rationale (Ayo 2012, pp. 102–103). Broom (2008, p. 130), among others, has pointed out that personal habits, choices, and lifestyle are disproportionately targeted in health promotion, considering that it is well known that the distribution of health and illnesses correlate significantly with, for example, class, gender, culture, ethnicity, and environmental issues that are mostly beyond the sole control of an individual (e.g. Guthman and DuPuis 2006; Palosuo *et al*. 2009). And yet because poverty, lack of education, and other social inequalities are also beyond the scope of existing healthcare systems and health policymakers, individuals remain and are re-established as the main agent of their health (Broom 2008, p. 131), irrespective of their circumstances. Concentration on the individual effectively depoliticises an issue that is thoroughly political. Although every aspect of health is political, healthism effectively personifies it in the individual, by making it a matter of personal choice.

Healthism appears to offer individuals a certain freedom in the form of choice, but this is more of an illusion than reality; since the power to determine the content of one's choice lies somewhere else (Rich, Harjunen, and Evans 2006). Nevertheless, healthism builds on the idea of free choice, and a level playing field is assumed. The assumption is that everyone has an equal opportunity to make the "right" and "rational" choices, for example, regarding their nutrition and exercise but, as mentioned above, the social norms regarding body size and one's "appearance of health" will, for instance, limit that choice. The ways of doing health "correctly" are restricted, and envision a certain type of healthy body, and in this respect, some people's choices are automatically seen as more valid than others. As Broom (2008, p. 132) has noted, what is considered rational or risky behaviour is also affected by the social status of the individual. Broom states that class, ethnic background, and gender play a role in what kind of health risks are deemed irrational. She notes that "health risks taken by ethnic minorities, working-class people and women are often construed as irrational, while the vices of middle-aged professional white men go unremarked, despite their substantial impact on individual or environmental health".

Broom (2008, p. 130) goes on to list at least three harmful consequences of focusing on individuals as targets of prevention and health promotion: (i) those who are ill become stigmatised; (ii) existing health service structures are not fully taken into account; and (iii) the surveillance of those individuals who are seen to be most in need of changing their unhealthy behaviour increases. Health status, whether assumed or real, should certainly not lead to stigmatisation, however, in the case of fatness it most certainly does. One of the most significant problems with targeting individuals is that, if they fail to adopt the desired habits and make the right choices, they are personally blamed for that failure and other factors that contribute to health are easily forgotten. Inequalities then are seen to appear as a result of individual differences, and not the social and cultural structures that maintain and produce them (Skeggs 2005, pp. 44–45). The emphasis on individual responsibility over health means that socioeconomic effects become obscured, as do those of class and gender.

Healthism is an ideology and practice that favours those who can dedicate time, money and effort to taking care of their bodies; it therefore both targets and is driven by the middle and well-to-do classes. In fact, Crawford (2006, p. 413) suggests that the rise in health and fitness consciousness has always been tightly connected to socioeconomic class, and particularly the professional middle classes' efforts to maintain their class position. Health and fitness has thus become an arena in which these classes have been able to re-establish their work ethic, by improving on their bodies.

> By making the body a task, the health conscious could demonstrate to self and others the core values that defined their class, reassuring themselves (and their employers) that they possessed the personal qualities that made them more equipped than their competitors for surviving the new economic realities.
>
> (Crawford 2006, p. 413)

Crawford goes on to note that at the same time as health and fitness boomed and the ideology of "personal responsibility" caught on, the middle classes were turning more and more towards right-wing politics and Reaganism in the US. He suggests that this personal responsibility over one's health was happening at the same time as there was criticism over alleged excessive public spending, and this combined to create a hostility towards welfare policy recipients. Since then, healthism combined with a neoliberal rationale has gradually transformed health into an arena of constant competition and personal achievement.

Fatness as a self-inflicted problem

Among others, Cheek (2008, p. 981) has observed that blaming individuals for their illness occurs most often when it is thought that the individual has the knowledge to make the right choices and be healthy. This tendency to see people as having conditions perceived to be a result of their own actions was observed by Goffman in the 1960s in his famous work on stigma and stigmatised identities (Goffman 1963). He noted that the stigma seemed to be stronger if it was thought to be self-inflicted and a consequence of a person's morals, lifestyle, or behaviour. Fatness of course is a prime example of one such characteristic that is commonly thought to be self-inflicted and thus one's own responsibility, which also makes it an obvious target for healthism and neoliberal governmentality.

For Goffman, a stigma was a characteristic that lowers the social status of individuals and has a negative effect on their social identity and self-perception. Goffman divided stigmatised groups into three classes: people with physical deformities, with character defects, or with what he called "tribal stigma" – relating to race, nationality and religion (Goffman 1963). Stigmatising characteristics could also be defined in terms of being either visible or invisible. Visible ones would be directly stigmatising, whereas invisible ones had the potential of becoming so if revealed. In this respect, fatness is obviously a very visible stigma, which has already been well documented (e.g. Harjunen 2009; Puhl and Brownell 2003), and the obesity epidemic discourse has further enhanced this (e.g. Boero 2012). If we use Goffmann's categorisation of different types of stigma, fat people are stigmatised both for their size – seen as a physical deformity, and their assumed moral weakness – seen as a character defect (e.g. Brink 1994). In other words, fat people are stigmatised for having a body that deviates from the accepted norm, and the body also says something about their moral or intellectual character too. But as was demonstrated in an earlier chapter, fat is always intersectional. Fat people are never just fat; they also belong to other groups of people. They can be women and fat, or working class and fat, disabled and fat, and so on. But the fat stigma seems to exacerbate the already precarious social position of these other groups (e.g. Herndon 2005). So for fat people who belong to an ethnic, religious, or other minority, the third category used by Goffman, the "tribal stigma", might also be applicable. In that case fatness means that these people would belong to all three of his categories of stigmatisation, and on both the visible and invisible levels.

The notion that fatness is self-inflicted is widespread and invariably appears in public discussions on the topic, no matter what context this is in (e.g.Valkendorff 2014) Fatness is assumed to be the result of bad choices made by individuals who must accept that they are responsible for the consequences.[1] A survey commissioned[2] by the Finnish broadcasting company YLE published in the spring of 2015 seemed to confirm this view. The purpose of the survey was to map out Finnish people's attitudes towards fatness. The majority of the 1,096 respondents thought that fatness is at least partially one's own fault and a result of one's own choices. A smaller number of people thought that it was completely self-inflicted (Rinta-Tassi 2015). In the same survey, people were asked about public healthcare costs in relation to fatness; and over half of the respondents (57 per cent) thought that public spending on tackling obesity should not be increased (Mommo 2015); although it was not reported how the current level of prevention was defined. I assume that it referred to the usual health promotion and weight-loss campaigns, medical consultations, monitoring of weight, diet-pill prescriptions, and so on. Interestingly, although many respondents were against spending more public money on the prevention and treatment of fatness, nevertheless more people were strongly against the suggestion that fat people should be charged more than others for healthcare services. In fact, 73 per cent of the respondents were completely against it.

The abovementioned survey was conducted in a context of a theme-day on YLE's network dedicated to the topic of fatness. A batch of five articles was published on the YLE website, and later that same evening (5 May 2015), a current affairs show about bariatric surgery was broadcast. The fact that bariatric surgery would be the primary topic of the theme-day was not evident from reading the articles that were published beforehand. However, the question about the costs of preventing and treating fatness is cast in a different light when put in the context of the costs of bariatric surgery. So far, at around 2,000 per year, the number of bariatric surgeries carried out in Finland is lower than in the other Nordic countries. This operation is carried out for free within the public healthcare system, and there are long queues for it as demand exceeds the supply. As a consequence, a growing number of private hospitals and clinics offer bariatric surgery, but it must be paid for mostly out of the patient's own pocket. The respondents' view that bariatric surgery should not be covered by public healthcare might reflect the opinion that fatness is a self-inflicted condition, and that therefore public funds should not be used to correct it.

In most discussions among non-experts, bariatric surgery is often seen as "the easy way out" or "cheating". The view seems to be that this is a quick-fix solution, and fat people should rather "suffer for their sins" (their irresponsible choices) and lose weight the hard way as a sort of punishment. Resorting to bariatric surgery does not fit the idea of the responsible individual who "does health" right and works consistently to maintain their body. The results of the survey seem to follow the logic of healthist neoliberal governmentality; people are perceived as personally responsible for creating their problem and should solve it themselves. And yet, at the same time, the premise of the survey and the subsequent television show also reflect the principles of economised and commercialised health services. A bariatric surgeon that was interviewed thought that the number of surgeries performed in Finland could at least be doubled (Miettinen 2015b); and of course, emphasising the need to perform more surgeries has clear marketing advantages for the private sector, where bariatric surgery costs around 10,000 euros.

A notable departure from the neoliberal line though, is the aforementioned respondents' opinion that fat people should not be charged more than other people for their healthcare. This last result is somewhat unexpected, as during the past decade the issue of making fat people pay more for their healthcare has been publicly taken up a number of times in Finland; thus this view seems to have some support in Finnish society (e.g. Harjunen 2012). For example, in 2005 the former prime minister of Finland, Esko Aho, and at the time the leader of the right-wing think tank, "Finnish Innovation Fund Sitra", suggested that people start paying tax for being either "too fat", for smoking, or for other behaviour that was considered detrimental to health and thus possibly costly to the public economy (Hukkanen 2005). Unsurprisingly, and in congruence with healthist governmentality, this risky behaviour is seen as a sign of personal, social, or moral incompetence, whereas doing sports is not considered risky, since it is assumed that one is involved in sports because of the possibly beneficial health effects, not for example, for the simple pleasure of the adrenalin rush that follows physical risk-taking. Sports injuries can be just as costly to care for as fatness-related illnesses and the most serious ones may even require life-long treatment; yet paying for these types of self-inflicted conditions is rarely questioned anywhere. Targeting some people and not others for their allegedly risky lifestyle choices goes against the principles of healthism in the sense that everyone is in danger of becoming ill all the time, and should act accordingly. However, since healthism is also a moral discourse, certain behaviours are perceived as riskier than others.

Wellness and women: buying normative femininity?

> Neoliberal government represents the population's wellbeing as intimately tied to individuals' abilities to make market principles the guiding values of their lives, to see themselves as products to create, sell, and optimize.
>
> (Ventura 2012, p. 2)

As discussed already in earlier chapters, the effects of the fat stigma are felt particularly acutely by women. In Western societies the normative idea of the healthy female body complies with whatever the prevalent ideals and norms are for beauty. This can be seen in the way aesthetic surgery is often marketed for women as contributing significantly to their overall health and well-being. In the same way, dieting is normalised into women's lives at least as much as a means for achieving a socially acceptable body as improving their health.

Since it has been shown that the effects of weight stigma are stronger for women, it is not a great surprise that women diet not only for health reasons

(Harjunen 2009; Sarlio-Lähteenkorva 1999). Indeed, most diet and weight loss advertising is targeted at women (Hänninen and Sarlio-Lähteenkorva 2005) in such a way that health and beauty become relatively indistinguishable.

This conflation of health with beauty has been further strengthened by the advent of "wellness". Alongside the conventional fields of healthcare, illness prevention, and health promotion, the eclectic field of "wellness" has emerged, bringing with it a host of new professionals and pseudo-professionals (see, for example, Cederström and Spicer 2015). Wellness was a term first introduced by Halbert L. Dunn (1961, pp. 4–5 in Kirkland 2014) and it has now become an umbrella term to describe a variety of practices that are said to enhance an individual's overall well-being. These practices may include elements from alternative medicine, particular nutritional regimes, exercises, and meditation, and it has been expanding. Wellness is a particularly commercialised branch of health, in which services, products, and programmes are marketed as a route to self-improvement and reaching one's full potential, with promises of a "new and improved you". Their claims to improve overall well-being often rely on emphasising the "balance" of their different components, by describing them in popular dualist terms as affecting both "body and mind" (Cederström and Spicer 2015). Because it is such a popular phenomenon, wellness is perhaps one of the best examples of how healthism and neoliberal rationale come together.

As we have seen, "doing health" has become a morally loaded and gendered activity for many. Indeed, health and well-being are defined very differently for men and women, as the following example should clearly show. In the autumn of 2011, I received a personalised promotional letter in the mail from a well-known Finnish private healthcare provider.

It was an invitation to a women's wellness evening that was marketed with the slogan "Time for Yourself, Wellness for You!", explaining that during the course of the evening, there would be talks given by a number of experts on such topics as "renewing your appearance" (from a plastic surgeon), "getting rid of your specs", "the secrets of beautiful skin", and "be all smiles with rapid teeth-whitening". I googled for more information, and noticed that for the same event in a nearby city, there was also a talk called "A Woman's Life: How Reconstructive Plastic Surgery can Help Mother Nature". In my letter, it was mentioned that after the talks, participants would have an opportunity to consult directly with these medical experts, including an oral hygienist, a plastic surgeon, a gynaecologist, a dermatologist, and a nutrition therapist. In other words, they would be able to give advice on how to improve my wellness regarding healthy teeth, teeth whitening, cosmetic surgery, skin care, and dieting. Assumedly, if I so wished, I could eventually buy these services from said private healthcare provider.

The invitation provoked some thought. At first, I was puzzled why I received such an invitation in the first place, as I had never been a client of the said clinic or pharmacy. But as soon as I noticed the tiny print in the bottom right corner of the invitation which indicated that my contact information had been obtained via Finland's Population Register Centre, I understood that my age was probably the key.

Although ageing was not specifically mentioned in the invitation (although "menopause" was mentioned), I deduced that I was on the company's mailing list because I had quite recently turned forty. In marketing terms, this indicates an age when a woman is assumed to have both financial resources and external incentive to spend money on her appearance or "wellness". It is commonplace that women from early middle-age onwards start to see the combined effects of sexism and ageism in working life and it makes sense to target this group with this kind of marketing. Many understandably feel that they cannot lose the competitive edge that a youthful, dynamic, attractive appearance can potentially give in today's labour market. The wellness evening was obviously a marketing event for the clinic and the pharmacy and the notion of wellness was obviously used deliberately and strategically as an umbrella term instead of health. Some of the treatments marketed here were primary healthcare services, but many fell into that vaguely defined category of "wellness" which can mean almost anything. Wellness is basically a broader, less scientific, less hierarchical, and more commercially flexible mode of (non-essential) healthcare. Predictably, most of the treatments marketed to women under this moniker seem to concentrate on the aesthetics and appearance of youthfulness, body size, and overall normative femininity and attractiveness. It is thus clearly as much about the appearance of the body as about actual health.

The logics of healthism and neoliberal governmentality are plainly at work here. A woman of certain age and socioeconomic position must surely spend money on her wellness or else she risks losing status. What happens if I do not want to invest in my wellness (as it is indeed considered an investment); or perhaps more precisely keep my appearance youthful-looking, attractive and thin? It is obvious that not complying with the norms of female appearance can put one in a precarious social position, and as long this threat is there, why risk it? As I have never seen an invitation for a men's wellness event, I do not know what kind of wellness is seen by this business as important for men over forty, but I think it is safe to assume that the "secrets of beautiful skin", which the invitation said was the topic the dermatologist was addressing, would probably not seem so attractive to men. It was also quite instructive that, although the term "health" was not used once in the invitation, it was clearly implied that by ensuring "wellness", normative ideals of feminine beauty would also be effortlessly met.

Disguising aesthetic treatments as wellness (or "health") is clearly a calculated marketing tool on the part of the service provider. The point is to attract clients who would have the money to pay for private services. But I also believe this phenomenon is a reflection of neoliberal (body) culture; in other words individualism, competition, and the aestheticisation of work. Sexism and ageism are realities that women have to deal with in their lives. Double standards regarding women's recruitment, for instance, are nothing new and women are well aware of this. It is not only their competence that counts, but also their appearance. In order to compete in the job market, women are invited to approach their bodies as an investment and regard themselves in entrepreneurial terms. Healthism as neoliberal governmentality helps to individualise sexism, and the same is happening with ageism. If you are not able to look young and dynamic, it is your own fault for neglecting to take better care of your body and appearance.

Are there limits to one's personal responsibility regarding appearance? Where does personal responsibility end; would I be morally accepted for not doing something towards my wellness that I nevertheless have the resources for? The notion of wellness is so broad and it can be used for any number of issues, and if it is then used interchangeably with the term "health", the possibilities for responsibilising the individual appear boundless. As I have attempted to show above, "free choice" in the healthist context is, in fact, rarely free. Only certain kinds of choices are morally and socially acceptable, namely those that can produce either a normative body or an improved version of it. It is doubtful that one would get much understanding for wanting breasts that drooped more, or having yellower teeth, even though we know that neither of these are likely pose any threat to our health. The fact is that normative expectations concerning the body and health will affect free choice whether these norms are social or medical in origin. When making these choices we cannot help but participate in the production and maintenance of gendered body norms; so it is important to ask at what point this "free choice" actually turns into simple obedience. In other words, at what point do we unwittingly choose to become a "docile body"?

Notes

1 In lay discussions fat people are habitually blamed for their own discrimination, which is sometimes seen as a deserved punishment for being fat.
2 The survey was conducted by commercial research company Taloustutkimus.

6 Money for your fat! Moral credit for disappearing fat

The way in which fatness is discussed is imbued with messages about its social, political, economic and moral meanings. Gard and Wright (2005) among others have noted this tendency to talk about a host of other issues while claiming to be talking about just "obesity". As I have maintained throughout this book, health, morals, and the neoliberal economy have become caught up with each other in a significant way in both the public discourse and public policies concerning fatness (see e.g. Harrison 2012; LeBesco 2011).

In this chapter, I will use one particular case to illustrate how these issues become tangled up with one another in subtle and not so subtle ways. I will show one way how fatness is portrayed as wasteful, excessive, unproductive, immoral, and expensive, and how the global economic discourse is woven into this portrayal. The case is a weight-loss campaign that ran in Finland in the spring of 2010, some years after the obesity epidemic discourse had started to become a major public discussion. My source material comes from press releases, newspaper articles and online articles that were written about the campaign before, during, and after it had run its course. I chose this particular case because the rhetoric that was used, the way it was organised, and the goals of the campaign seemed to be unusually saturated with prejudices and assumptions about fatness and fat people based on cultural stereotypes and a simplistic understanding of the issue, in terms of both its causes and consequences. The campaign is also a good example of the ways in which questions of health, morals, and economics intersect in the discussion concerning fat and fat bodies.

The "Literacy in Fat" campaign

So this is how the story begins: in late 2009 it was announced that an anonymous Finnish private sponsor had donated ten million euros (approximately twelve million dollars) for a weight loss campaign that was, I assume deliberately and provocatively, called "Literacy in Fat", although the Finnish term for fat was perhaps more derogatory (*Läskillä lukutaitoa*). I first became aware of the campaign from one of the Finnish tabloid papers that had written a short piece about it. The title of the article was "Sponsor Buys Human Fat" (Heiskanen 2009). Subsequently, I looked up the campaign's press release, published on the website of the National Institute for Health and Welfare (*Terveyden ja hyvinvoinnin laitos* 29 December 2009)[1] (translation by HH).

"Literacy in Fat": a weight loss campaign for the benefit of teacher education in Nepal

> Upon the request of a private citizen, the National Institute for Health and Welfare of Finland will coordinate a weight loss campaign in the spring of 2010, whereby said private citizen will buy fat at the price of 15€ per kilogram from people who are permanent residents in Finland. The moneys collected will be donated toward developing teacher education in Nepal. Only people who are of legal age can participate in the campaign. Only kilograms that are overweight will be tallied, so kilograms lost that take the weight below the threshold of ideal weight will not be tallied. The sponsor of the campaign is committed to buying lost weight to the maximum amount of ten million euros. The buying of fat will take place throughout 2010. Finland has supported the education sector in Nepal for a long time. The Ministry of Foreign Affairs will monitor that the moneys will be used appropriately. The sponsor of the campaign has expressed a wish that the Finnish Evangelical Lutheran Church would organise the weighing of participants, with the wish that as many parishes or other partners as possible offer the possibility for people to "sell their fat" as follows: dieters who want to take part in the campaign ("sellers of fat") will go to a place appointed by the parish for weighing on 7 February at the latest. The parish will register their name, date of birth, starting weight, height, and the lowest ideal weight of the participant. In May 2010, the person will return to the parish, be weighed again and the new weight and the amount of "bought fat" will be registered. The parishes will then send this information on to the National Institute for Health and Welfare. The amount of money that will be donated to teacher education in Nepal will be based on this information.

The idea of the campaign seemed simple enough; people were encouraged to join *en masse* in a nationwide, competitive weight-loss campaign and try to lose as much weight or "flab" as possible in a period of three months.[2] For every kilogram, or couple of pounds, in weight lost, the sponsor would pay fifteen euros towards improving teacher education in Nepal.

What made this particular campaign stand out from other weight loss campaigns, apart from the provocative title, and the large sum of money being donated towards it, was the fact that the anonymous sponsor had managed to persuade a very authoritative trio of major national institutions to back the campaign. Not only were the Finnish National Institute for Health and Welfare, and Ministry for Foreign Affairs involved, but also the Evangelical Lutheran Church – the state church of Finland.[3] These three institutions are responsible for health policy and health education in Finland, the country's relationship with the international community, and the religious and moral guidance of the nation respectively.

Involvement by these institutions not only gave credibility to the campaign but also enforced an understanding that this kind of attitude to fatness, this approach to weight loss, health promotion, and perhaps even international development was approved by the highest authorities in Finland. These three did not simply represent the highest level of expertise in their own field. Whether it was the intention of the sponsor or not, it is difficult to ignore that they were perhaps also chosen for their representative power. It is enticing to think that in addition to the concrete roles these institutions were allotted, all three were also given symbolic roles in the campaign representing health and wellbeing, aid and charity, and ethics and morals.

Continuing with this line of thought, the anonymous private "sponsor" could also be seen as a representative of the world of business and private enterprise and other members of the population. It can be assumed that, to some extent at least, the sponsor's personal worldview played a significant part in how the campaign was organised.[4] Besides funding it, the press release also mentions that it was the sponsor's specific request that the Evangelical Lutheran Church participate in the campaign as the trustworthy body that registers the weights.

It might have been the case that the National Institute for Health and Welfare (known then as the National Public Health Institute) agreed to take part in the campaign because the promised funding was so substantial, or because it had taken part in something similar before. Previous to this, in reaction to the obesity epidemic, it had coordinated a nationwide weight-loss campaign from 2003 until 2006, in collaboration with the Finnish Red Cross (SPR), called the "Million Kilogram Gig".[5] Participants were weighed at the beginning and end of the campaign; received information brochures about nutrition and exercise; and a sum equivalent to the kilograms lost was paid via UNICEF towards fighting child starvation in Africa.

Moralising prejudice in the campaign

Had it not been for its intentionally crude title, the campaign might have come across as a more charitable one. As noted above, the Finnish word for fat used in the title is actually quite an offensive term, the original meaning of which is a reference to animal fat, specifically pig fat, or lard. Tellingly, when I checked the synonyms for the word "*läski*" in a reputable online dictionary,[6] I got a list of thirteen words, all of which are in common use to abuse fat people. The original meaning of the word as "pig fat" only came up in the examples of how to use the word; all the other meanings given were abusive.

The use of a colloquial word that has a well-known pejorative connotation in the name of the campaign was clearly intentional. It might have been an attempt to gain publicity, or a strategy to appeal to a certain segment of the population, such as people who are put off by formal or scientific language and public health promotion, and who prefer "straight talk". Either way, using the word *läski* identifies this as not just a weight-loss campaign but as one that was essentially anti-fat and fat people. The choice of the name conveys the message that fat people do not deserve the same kind of respect as others, least of all for being fat. In fact, I cannot recall any other health drives that would have chosen to disrespect their target population in this manner. It could be that the name was inspired by an earlier weight-loss campaign in 2007 and launched by the biggest Finnish newspaper *Helsingin Sanomat*, called "Läskitalkoot" or "Fat Bee" (Kyrölä 2007). However, that particular campaign received so much criticism for its paternalistic tone and one-sided approach that it would not have served as a very good normative example.[7]

Since "fat" in the Finnish context is not a word that has yet been reclaimed to any great extent, it is safe to assume that it was probably chosen to shock and shame into action the people it was trying to target. The word is obviously used in a negative sense and as a slur. Name-calling is a classic strategy used to bully fat people (e.g. Harjunen 2009). It is assumed that fat people should be ashamed of their bodies and themselves, and indeed, that it needs to be pointed out that they are fat. Blaming the target of abuse for their own discrimination is a commonplace occurrence that is recognised by many marginalised groups. The target of bullying is supposed to draw the conclusion that it is their responsibility to change, if they want to escape this abuse. The use of bullying tactics to encourage dieting is unfortunately not a new thing. The stigma of weight is sometimes even seen as a useful tool to motivate people to lose weight (e.g. Critser 2004).

When the campaign was launched, the obesity epidemic discourse had already become the dominant cultural frame to discuss fatness. It clearly provided the inspiration and politics behind the "Literacy in Fat" campaign.[8] According to the obesity epidemic discourse and its trademark amalgamation of healthism and neo-liberal thought, fatness is first and foremost a moral issue concerning people's medical health. As we have seen, the campaign was "open to all", and yet there were some guidelines to be followed. Body Mass Index (BMI) was being used as the means for measuring weight loss in the campaign. Those whose weight was in the underweight category to begin with or whose weight loss would result in them becoming underweight (in BMI terms) would not be able to take part in the campaign. In other words, the lowest the participants could go with their weight was the lowest threshold of the normal weight range; everything above that threshold, even within the normal range, was fat that could be lost for the purposes of the campaign. Interestingly, there was no indication of any limit for the amount of weight one was allowed to lose in three months, although it is well established in research that losing weight fast is neither healthy nor sustainable (e.g. Sarlio-Lähteenkorva 1999). From this it is clear that the principle of the campaign was to lose as much fat as possible in a limited period of time, which seems to go against everything that medical experts, the National Institute for Health and Welfare, and other authorities involved with weight loss usually advise. Not only does this encourage unhealthy weight-loss methods, and usually results only in short-term weight loss but it also results in weight cycling, when any weight lost is soon put on again. Nevertheless, this is in line with the popular purely mechanical understanding of weight loss and its benefits, and a conception of health that sees dieting as normal and focuses only on weight. Any weight loss is thus good weight loss, unless it is due to starvation and eating disorders that result in becoming underweight.

But this obesity epidemic discourse-styled moral judgement is not just implicit in the title of the campaign; it is implicit throughout. Fat phobia or anti-fat sentiment is being not simply camouflaged, but paraded as a health concern, with a juxtaposition being made between excessive First World lifestyles and genuine needs in the Third World, with a replication of uneasy colonial relationships from the past, which is only augmented by the Church being involved so that fat is seen as a sin that needs to be confessed. The subtext of the campaign is clear; the unfair First World surplus, embodied in people's fat, would be literally exchanged for money so that deprived Third World children could receive a better education. Based on the articles written about the campaign, fat is construed as a sign of greed, selfishness, and over-consumption, thus drawing on an already established stereotype. This simplistic view of fat people is also reflected in the juxtaposition between First and Third Worlds, which has long been used in everyday discussions by experts and lay people alike about starvation and fatness, which to many seem clearly linked. In fact, in the early 2000s, in one of the first public debates I ever took part in about fatness on Finnish TV, a medical doctor who had been pre-interviewed for the talk show drew a similar analogy as if there was cause and effect relationship between people getting fatter in the West, and starvation in "Africa" (the term was used to refer to the whole continent). The campaign applies this same simplistic logic by buying the excess fat and donating that excess fat in the form of money to, in this case, "educationally undernourished" children. The fat person is clearly the embodiment of Western excess, and the simplistic solution is that, as soon as this excess has been dealt with, global inequality will be a little bit better.

As discussed earlier, body fat has for a long time had a symbolic value attached to it. In popular folklore, fatness has been associated with the vices of laziness, greed, and gluttony. Fat people are seen to be hedonists with a weak will, and lacking virtuous characteristics such as intelligence, self-control, discipline, and diligence.

Choosing a church or a local parish building as the location for weighing seems to add to the moral implications of fatness, even though fat is anyway commonly understood as a kind of moral failure even outside the religious context. An assumed gluttonous relationship with food, in other words, lack of control when faced with the temptation of food, persists as a popular explanation for people's fatness. Eating, especially the hedonistic enjoyment and consumption of food, is frequently talked about in terms of sin in everyday conversations. In contrast, dieting and refusal to eat are seen as virtuous and morally commendable. In some religious communities this sinfulness of fatness is taken very seriously. As Gerber (2011) has shown, some evangelical Christians in the US believe God hates fatness and so weight-loss programmes are offered to their members. The sponsor's wish that fat (sinful) people be weighed in a morally loaded religious location seems deliberate. It bears more than a passing similarity to Catholic confession: the fat person comes to the church to be weighed at the start of the three-month period, and to confess the sin of being fat, repentance follows, after which comes the second weighing and absolution of the fat person's sins.

Foucault, of course, has written about the role of confession in becoming a self-disciplined subject (e.g. 1990); and indeed the moral judgement inherent in reporting one's weight is woven into this campaign. The fat body is perceived as a manifestation of the world's moral corruption, greed and excess. However, fat can be given an exchange value. If fat is exchanged for money, which will then be used to bring knowledge and a safer future to undereducated Third World children, it seems that fat can miraculously be transformed into an agent for good. The other reason this idea might capture the public's imagination is that, by simplistically contrasting the developed and developing worlds in terms of "obese First World helps undereducated (and possibly undernourished) children of the Third World", it appears as if the participants who are losing their fat are somehow metaphorically "feeding" those children. By contrasting developed and developing world, this campaign aims to teach a moral.

The commodification of fat

What is happening here is the commodification of fat, and as is usually the case when this happens, it is commodified through negation. Fat is valuable only when it is disappearing or assumed to be disappearing. The undesirability of fat is the basis for a myriad of plans, programmes, and products that have been designed to help in its obliteration. The fight against fat is a machine in perpetual motion. The value of fat lies in the consumerism of those that strive to lose it, but rarely do, and so the wheel keeps spinning. By giving fat a monetary value, the campaign promotes thinking about fat in terms of financial value, costs, and investment. This is one way that one's body becomes thought about in monetary terms.

Commodification of the human body has a long history (Sharp 2000). Bodies and various parts of them have been bought and sold for slavery, and they have been exploited for labour in other ways. Female bodies have been sold for marriage and prostitution; nowadays the female body can even be rented out for surrogate pregnancy, or just its eggs. Reading the press release of the weight-loss campaign, it struck me that in addition to using the language of buying and selling, the terms "donate" and "donor" were both also in use. These are terms normally used for people who donate their organs or other biological materials without compensation, and often for altruistic reasons; however, there is also a market for these things. The recent rapid development in the fields of biomedicine and bio-technologies has meant that a wide variety of biological materials and services are now available commercially. For example, organs, tissues, and other biological materials such as semen can be bought and sold (Goold *et al.* 2014, p. 3).

This development has brought along new ethical dilemmas. The body is increasingly discussed in terms of property, and questions concerning the use, commercialisation and possession of the body and its parts are manifold. Understanding the body as property raises the question of possession and ownership, i.e. who owns the rights to a body, and who controls it (Goold *et al.* 2014). It also casts the position of "donor" in a new light. I am confident when using such a term in the context of donating human materials, neither the sponsor of the campaign nor the affiliated authorities were referring to any discussions about the difference between the concepts of "gift" and "commodity" in any serious way. However, the fact that these terms were used, no matter how light-heartedly, leads us to questions about the nature of fat as a human biological material that can be donated. For the sake of argument, however, I will consider the participants in this campaign as "fat donors" and think about what the donation of fat could signify.

When we talk about the body as property in the biomedical sense, we usually talk about those parts of the body that are seen "useful". They might, for example, improve somebody's functionality and mobility, create possibilities for them that they otherwise would not have, perhaps even save someone's life. This "usefulness" means these body parts are not only valuable for the patient, but also valuable as commodities in that they have exchange value. I am interested here in the commodification of bodies or body parts that are not thought to have any usability or exchange value. Those bodies and parts of the body that are seen as unusable, invaluable or excessive, such as fat tissue, are rarely discussed in this context.

The "Literacy in Fat" campaign obviously did not deal with buying actual adipose fat tissue. It was given a symbolic value, and this was then purchased. Monetary reward was paid as compensation for destroying something not thought to be of any value to the human body. The "payment" was made in the hope that after losing fat the body – and the person – would be healthier. The alchemy of this medico–moral–economic exchange is that it transforms something immoral and destructive into something good; thereby turning the fat body into a donor body. In the process, the previously scorned and immoral fat body turns into a virtuous one in a process that requires the immaterialisation of fat, so that more money can be given to charity to pay for socially valuable knowledge and education.

In this campaign, the fat body, which is usually construed as a costly body, has been turned by a curious twist of alchemy into a body that can be used for "moral profit". In other words, the moral value of losing weight has been quantified in economic terms. In the end, this process of buying and selling fat marks the fat body and fat as something intrinsically immoral that can only be transformed into something moral and honourable when it has been lost. And to best achieve this, we are of course expected to use (i.e. consume) some dietary or weight-loss product or service; just as a neoliberal health programme would have us do.

The campaign appears to contain and represent most of the themes that have been discussed in this book, namely how fatness can be construed not only as a health issue, but also as one of morality and economics too. These three distinct strands of discussion become interwoven together in a way that gives a "natural" impression of progression (and association); however, it is still very much a construction. Essentially, it is a prime demonstration of the manner in which hegemonic discourses are produced, maintained, and reinforced. In this case, the hegemonic fat discourse is being produced via an interesting combination of expertise and popular folklore.

It can be argued that the campaign commodifies the fat body (and other bodies too) and consolidates and thus naturalises a link between the body and the economy. Thinking of bodies in terms of its parts and assigning those body parts monetary value leads to an increasingly refined commodification of the physical body. The body that was previously simply measured in terms of its physical qualities (height, weight, circumference, fat percentage, etc.) now also has an economic and moral value assigned to those physical qualities. This is neoliberal governmentality in a nutshell.

In the end, the campaign was only a moderate success. Not all the money available to "buy fat" got spent. In fact, at the end of the campaign, the sponsor decided to pay thirty euros instead of fifteen per kilogram of lost fat, and still only 1.4 million euros, just 14 per cent, of the possible ten million euro fund was used. According to the news on YLE (14 June 2010), the national broadcasting corporation in Finland, 23,500 Finns were weighed at the beginning of the campaign and 60 per cent of those returned for the second weighing. So approximately 14,200 participants lost about 48,100 kilograms during the campaign. Unsurprisingly, considering gendered body norms and the pressure to stay thin, 80 per cent of the participants were women. After the campaign, the sponsor said that the campaign had been a 70 per cent success, "encouraged by popular feedback, the participants' enthusiasm, and their lighter feeling and step". One could speculate whether the campaign would have been more of a success, however, if the financial incentives used had gone at least partly towards the efforts of the participants.

As is well known, long-term weight-loss remains an elusive goal. New methods are continually being introduced, and recently the usefulness of financial incentives has been explored. For example, employers and insurers, as part of workplace wellness programmes, have tried encouraging people to remain within the "normal weight range" by offering them monetary rewards; so far the results have been discouraging or inconclusive. In one study (Kullgren *et al.* 2013), however, financial incentives were found to have a positive effect. The results showed that those who were paid for reaching a weight-loss goal (at the end of a month) lost more weight than those who were just attending weigh-ins. When an extra cash price to be split among a team that had lost the most weight was added, people lost even more weight. However, in a more recent survey article that looked into financial incentives for weight loss, the conclusion was that it cannot be satisfactorily concluded that they work, especially not one-off incentives, and there is a need for a bigger study (Paloyo *et al.* 2011).

It would be tempting to think that the reason only such a relatively small number of people participated in the campaign was because people were uncomfortable with the clumsy rhetoric of the campaign and its barely hidden moralistic undertones. And what about the 40% who started the campaign and who dropped out before the finish? It is most likely that what happened is what normally happens with crash diets – they fail.

Notes

1 Original Press Release from National Institute for Health and Welfare's website: *"website: ess Release from National Institute for Health and Welfaresmall nu* Suomalaisen yksityishenkilön aloitteesta Terveyden ja hyvinvoinnin laitos (THL) koordinoi keväällä 2010 kansallisen laihdutuskampanjan, jossa kyseinen yksityishenkilö "ostaa Suomessa vakinaisesti asuvien henkilöiden läskiä 15 €/kg" Nepalissa tapahtuvan opettajankoulutuksen hyväksi. Kampanjaan saavat osallistua vain täysi-ikäiset henkilöt. Ihannepainon alarajan alittavia kiloja ei lasketa mukaan. Kampanjan taustahenkilö sitoutuu lunastamaan laihdutuskiloja enintään 10 miljoonalla eurolla. Lunastus tapahtuu vuoden 2010 aikana. Suomi on tukenut pitkään Nepalin opetussektoria. Ulkoasiainministeriö valvoo, että rahat menevät oikeaan kohteeseen ja seuraa niiden käyttöä. Kampanjan taustahenkilö toivoo, että Suomen evankelisluterilaiset seurakunnat voisivat olla mukana punnitusten järjestämisessä. Toiveena on, että mahdollisimman moni seurakunta tai muu yhteistyökumppani voisi tarjota alueellaan mahdollisuuden "läskin myyntiin". Se tapahtuu lahjoittajan toiveen mukaan esimerkiksi seuraavasti: Kampanjaan osallistuva laihduttaja ("läskin myyjä") menee esimerkiksi seurakunnan ilmoittamana ajankohtana, 7.2.2010 mennessä, seurakunnan osoittamaan paikkaan punnittavaksi. Seurakunta kirjaa myyjän nimen, syntymäajan, alkupainon, pituuden sekä ihannepainon alarajan. Toukokuussa 2010 sama henkilö menee jälleen samaan seurakuntaan sen ilmoittamana ajankohtana, jolloin hänet punnitaan uudelleen ja loppupaino sekä "ostettavan läskin" määrä kirjataan. Seurakunnat toimittavat THL:lle yhteistiedot, minkä perusteella Nepalin opettajankoulutuksen tukisumma määräytyy. THL tulee tammikuun alussa yhteistyökumppaneiden kanssa sovitun mukaisesti tiedottamaan kampanjasta yksityiskohtaisemmin ja antamaan verkkosivuillaan seurakunnille ohjeet punnituksista ja laihdutuskilojen ("ostettavan läskin") ilmoittamisesta sille 7.6.2010 mennessä. THL kehottaa seurakuntia tarvittaessa pyytämään punnituksen järjestelyihin apua paikkakuntansa terveyskeskukselta tai sydänyhdistykseltä. THL on saanut tiedoksi kampanjan taustana olevan ostositoumuksen".

2 Weighing only needed to take place *within* the dates given for the start and end of the campaign.

3 The bigger of two state churches in Finland. Approximately 80 per cent of the population are members.

4 This is based on unconfirmed information that was received from a former employer of the National Institute for Health and Welfare. My own investigation into the identity of the sponsor only revealed that he was a wealthy self-made businessman and a sports enthusiast.

5 "The Million Kilo Gig" (*Miljoonan kilon keikka*) ran from 2003 to 2006. The campaign was organised three times a year, each "gig" lasting for four months.

6 HS dictionary: http://www.sanakirja.org/search.php?id=105862&l2=3 1.

7 I have no substantive knowledge on who chose the name, However, I suspect the wealthy sponsor probably had a part to play, as they came up with the idea for the campaign in the first place (personal information).

8 The sponsor was apparently worried about the obesity epidemic and (supposedly) growing obesity rate in Finland and wanted to do something about it.

7 Postfeminism, fatness, and female body norms

Throughout this book I have argued that neoliberal rationale influences the way we think, talk about, organise, and govern our bodies, and that neoliberal rationale has come to underlie our understanding and treatment of the fat body. Bodies are affected by neoliberal policy in a number of ways and in various fields of life. I have indicated some of the ways in which the neoliberal rationale becomes embedded in the health and body discourses and practices we live by. In this chapter, I will specifically focus on gender, and how it relates to the mix already discussed.

Rosalind Gill (2007, p. 164) has suggested that neoliberalism is gendered from the start and that women are constructed as its ideal subjects. Gill argues that what is known as postfeminism, if understood as a specific sensibility, is also a major contributor in creating loyal neoliberal female subjects: putting the emphasis on individual responsibility, self-regulation, and free choice in applying femininity to the body. Others scholars, like Dworkin and Wachs (2009) and Heywood (2007), have also observed in their respective works how the neoliberal rationale affects the way gendered bodies are represented in the media, how they are interpreted, and the demands they set on the female embodied subject.

But is the postfeminist sensibility that Gill identifies in media representations of women and their bodies perhaps a neoliberal expression of feminism? Is the postfeminist female subject neoliberal or is the neoliberal female subject that is constructed simply appropriating feminism? I have two main questions relating to the relationship of neoliberalism, feminism and the fat body: first, how are norms of the female body moulded by neoliberal culture; and second, what is the position of the fat body in a feminist landscape that seems to embrace neoliberal rationality? Before going further into these relationships, I will first briefly discuss feminist politics concerning body norms in order to provide some background for that discussion.

From sexual objects to empowered agents?

Questions relating to the female body's appearance have been recognised as political in feminist scholarship since at least the early 1970s (e.g. Chernin 1981; Millman 1980; Orbach 1998 [1977; 1982]). An abundance of academic literature on female body norms and ideals, their origins, consequences, and oppressive nature has thus been published over the past forty years. It has been well established that body norms (especially those relating to body size) are stricter for women than for men and that there is a strong pressure on women to have a normative body. Women's body norms are constantly monitored both privately and publicly, and transgressions of them often result in social penalties of some kind (Bordo 1993; Wolf 1991).

Early feminist scholarship on body norms and appearance focused on women's body and beauty ideals; with the thin norm ("tyranny of slenderness" as Chernin called it) and eating disorders especially in focus (Chernin 1981). The sexual objectification of women's bodies was identified and critiqued – particularly in visual culture. Laura Mulvey's (1975) notion of the "male gaze" that constructs women as objects for males to look at provided an important tool for the feminist analysis of media images, and these were identified as a major source of women's dissatisfaction with their bodies. Although the sexist and sexualising portrayal of women in the media and society was seen to be an integral part of the problem, reasons for women's body image issues were often looked for within the individual, not the society. Psychological explanations were popular. For example, eating disorders were interpreted as a reaction to oppressive body norms. Women were said to deal with body image problems by internalising them and taking this out on their bodies (e.g. Chernin 1981; Orbach 1978). Interestingly, women's eating disorders were interpreted both as a result of these oppressive body norms and as a form of resistance against them (Bordo 1993; Saukko 1995).

It was not just eating disorders such as *anorexia nervosa* or *bulimia nervosa* that were explained by psychological reasons; women's fatness too was discussed in similar terms. For example Susie Orbach's famous work *Fat is a Feminist Issue* (1978) approached fatness as an eating disorder. Orbach's views in particular have been critiqued by feminist fat studies researchers for equating fatness with an eating disorder resulting from a trauma, which effectively individualises and pathologises fatness and the fat body. This supports the medicalisation of fatness and distracts attention from the very real structural and social inequalities that contribute to the fat stigma, and the very real social discrimination fat women experience due to their body size (e.g. Cooper 1998; Harjunen 2009).

Women's body norms and appearance have continued to be the focus of feminist studies on the body. The thin norm in particular has been investigated. Body norms and beauty ideals have been considered a part of patriarchal culture; the aim of which is to create a type of femininity that complies with patriarchal power relations and gender roles. In her seminal work, *The Beauty Myth*, Naomi Wolf famously connected women's pursuit of thinness and dieting to power and control (1991, p. 187). She wrote that "a culture fixated on female thinness is not an obsession about female beauty, but an obsession about female obedience. Dieting is the most potent political sedative in women's history; a quietly mad population is a tractable one". According to Wolf, the thin ideal and dieting are used to control women. This resonates strongly with Foucault's notion of how "docile bodies" are produced.

In another key feminist work on body norms, *Unbearable Weight: Feminism, Western Culture, and the Body* (1993), Susan Bordo looked into the role that popular and consumer cultures have in constructing femininity and female bodies discursively and materially. Bordo seems to agree with Wolf in saying that the normative demands and expectations concerning the look, size, and shape of the female body have never been simply about appearance. Control and regulation of the body are also connected to the regulation of women's agency and social freedom. Bordo (1993) suggests, inspired by Foucauldian thought on the body and power, that normalising techniques concerning the female body have aimed at producing not only normatively acceptable femininity but also a passive and submissive role for women in society. But, significantly, Bordo does *not* view women's commitment to body shaping as just a response to patriarchal culture and its demands. Even though women's own discipline and regulation of their bodies seems to be in compliance with patriarchal social norms and structures, there are other reasons for them to engage in beauty and body work: women also really do gain pleasure and embody experiences of freedom and empowerment through them (1993, pp. 27–29). Along the same lines, Heyes (2006) has suggested that this sense of control and pleasure gained by becoming a "self-disciplined" subject probably goes some way to explain the popularity of dieting.

This apparent paradox of "choosing" to engage in practices that ultimately reinforce and tighten body norms for all women continues to fascinate feminist academics, and is clearly at the centre of the discussion concerning feminism, gender, the body, and neoliberalism (Gill 2007). Different body practices, from the use of cosmetics to exercise, dieting, body building, and cosmetic surgery have been reassessed and to some extent rehabilitated, so they are no longer simply seen as signs of women's oppression or "false consciousness", but also as actions of an autonomous and empowered subject and an expression of female agency (Davis 1995, p. 159; Kinnunen 2008).

Nevertheless, we need to ask why it is pleasurable or empowering to become a self-disciplined subject through body work such as dieting. In the light of the discussions in the previous chapters of this book concerning healthism, gender, and wellness, it seems that such experiences of empowerment and pleasure are constructed as a part of the practice of self-governing and becoming a self-disciplined subject, and are not separate from it. In fact, women are actively encouraged to think of self-governance and disciplining the body as sources of empowerment and pleasure. This seems to indicate the creation of a type of embodied female agency and feminism which has incorporated discipline and self-regulation as part of its very core. This shift in the notion of what women's bodies represent and how they are experienced has been discussed in recent years in the context of "postfeminism".

How to build a neoliberal girl

The 1990s saw the emergence of a new kind of female subject that seemed to embrace commercialism and embody neoliberal subjectivity (Gonick 2006, pp. 15–17). This new female subject became familiar for many through popular culture and such pop-feminist notions as "Girl Power", popularised by the British pop group the Spice Girls. Although the slogan itself originated in the more political and radical feminist "Riot grrrl" movement earlier the same decade, wider audiences are most likely to associate "Girl Power" with the Spice Girls (Gonick 2006, p. 9). It seemed to be first and foremost about attitude, and the empowerment of girls and young women through assertiveness and individualism. The five members of the Spice Girls were basically active, confident, noisy, and fun-loving.

Alongside the Spice Girls, the popular television series *Sex and the City* (SATC) has often been used as another example of the 1990s "new female subject" and postfeminism (e.g. Gerhard 2005). Its four female protagonists were portrayed as modern independent women – empowered and sexually liberated (Gill 2007). Both of these popular cultural phenomena have been commended for promoting feminist values, by putting an emphasis on women's independence, on the importance of a work ethic, on loyalty between women, on feminism in general, and for being an open unabashed expression of sexuality and sexual desire. Girl Power and SATC were both very popular and hailed for representing a form of feminism that was fresh, fun, and sexy (Gonick 2006), but what was new in their feminism? It seems that a large part of their success was due to a skilful appropriation and commodification of feminism. Their "girl power" was clearly capitalist from the outset, as although it drew from feminism, it was also unashamedly commercial in its approach. It promoted independence and empowerment while at the same time selling a commodity and commodified feminism to a young female audience (Driscoll 1999, p. 178).

Meanwhile, the feminism of the protagonists in *Sex and the City* also drew from consumerism (albeit from the higher end). Identity building via consumer culture was an essential part of the show and of the women's subjectivity and agency. In particular, SATC promoted an idea of femininity that could be acquired through the consumption of products and services provided by the beauty, fashion, and dietary industries. In consumer culture, the market that capitalises on women's physical insecurities also portrays itself as the means to get rid of those anxieties, and as a way for an empowered woman to lead a successful life. The new feminist subjects that girl power and SATC were championing were commodified to the core. They might appear feminist (at least on the surface), but this feminism is at the same time deeply engaged with capitalism and consumer culture and is at least partially its product. In this respect they seem to embody many of the ideals of neoliberalism.

The Spice Girls and SATC can be viewed as examples of the "postfeminist sensibility" that Rosalind Gill identifies in a 2007 article "Postfeminist Media Culture: Elements of a sensibility". In this article, Gill explored the construction of femininity and the female body in the media and popular culture of the early 2000s, taking as her starting point the concept of postfeminism and looking into contemporary media's representation of women and their bodies. At this point, it should be pointed out that there is no agreement on the meaning of postfeminism; some think it refers to the end of feminism, others to a new stage in feminism. Then there is Gill's interpretation of postfeminism as a neoliberal phenomenon, which clearly resonates with my own understanding of the construction of the gendered body in contemporary culture. She proposes that postfeminism could be seen as a "sensibility" that that draws from present-day culture and is made up of a number of issues that link with second-wave feminism. Thus, postfeminism would not just be an epistemological break, or historical shift to a third wave of feminism, nor a backlash against feminism as previously presented (Gill 2007, p. 148).

Understanding postfeminism as a sensibility would seem to explain both this new type of female subject and the shift in the ideas of feminism, the female body, and femininity portrayed by the Spice Girls and SATC examples given above. Among the typical characteristics of postfeminist discourse, Gill describes femininity as a bodily property, the shift from objectification to subjectification, and the emphasis on self-surveillance, monitoring, and discipline, not just of the body, but of the self. Gill goes on to list notions of individualism; choice and empowerment; the prevalence of the makeover paradigm; the return of naturally essentialising sexual difference; the sexualisation of culture; and an emphasis on consumerism and commodification of these differences as notable features of postfeminist discourse (Gill 2007, p. 149).

Based on her analysis of various popular culture and media phenomena from magazines (men and women's), television shows, film, and literature, Gill comes to the conclusion that the constructs of femininity and the female body in contemporary media culture are replete with messages that are uncannily similar to the ones typically associated with a neoliberal rationale – particularly the notions of individual responsibility, self-monitoring, and free choice. Gill suggests that one of the major influences on postfeminism is in fact, neoliberal discourse. In both postfeminist and neoliberal discourses individuals are portrayed as "entrepreneurial actors", whose every action is made out to be a choice, that is, a rational decision the results of which the individual alone is responsible for (Gill 2008, p. 436).

Popular media constructs the postfeminist female subject as someone who is autonomous, in control, and sexually empowered; and yet she is also continually monitoring and objectifying herself as a heterosexual male fantasy (Gill 2007). In other words, while postfeminist discourse appears to put the emphasis on women's autonomous choice, agency, and their empowerment, what women are free to choose from and what should make them feel empowered are curiously the same things as the archetypal heterosexual male fantasy – a type of body that is considered sexy and always sexually available (Gill 2008, p. 437). This would seem to reinforce rather than dismantle the notion that the female body is for the male gaze to enjoy and control. In this respect, the major difference in the representation of women in postfeminist media is that now women can "choose" whether or not to actively objectify themselves in the name of empowerment.

Gill's reading of the postfeminist media discourse challenges the idea that body work done allegedly for oneself and one's own pleasure is feminist or empowered. In this sense, postfeminist media discourse has not been able to "reclaim" the female body. Although packaged slightly differently as body work being women's own choice, the expectations for the female body do not ostensibly deviate from sexist expectations of the female body; that is, women need to be young, thin, pretty, and heterosexual to be desirable. The postfeminist body empowerment discourse thus seems to outline yet another normative requirement for women's bodies, a patriarchal reading of an empowered sexuality and sexy appearance, both categories of which exclude, for instance, those female bodies that are deemed too big, too old, or simply too different. In this way, postfeminism is yet another form of neoliberal governmentality, the aim of which is to turn women into entrepreneurial subjects and self-sufficient individuals.

Neoliberal surveillance and control

As has already been amply demonstrated, the female body has been the target of oppressive body norms, and patriarchal social and moral control for a long time (e.g. Bartky 1990; Bordo 1993). So has anything changed? In Chapter 5 I wrote about the effects of healthism and its relationship with neoliberal governmentality and how these influence our perception of health, healthy bodies, and health practices – self-governance and working on the body become a social and moral necessity. Monitoring and surveillance of the female body has intensified. According to Gill (2007, p. 155), this happens in three ways: (i) there is a dramatic increase in self-surveillance by women, accompanied by a denial of such regulation; (ii) this surveillance is extended over entirely new spheres of life and even regards intimate conduct; and (iii) there is a focus on the psychological, with a need to transform oneself and "remodel one's interior life".

These three modes of self-surveillance are visible in popular culture discourse, but also outside the media. All the methods of surveillance mentioned are easily discernible in the present-day approach to the fat body both in the media and in women's material lives: the duty to self-monitor and discipline (if necessary) and to constantly improve the flawed self and body is certainly a familiar one (Harjunen 2009; Kyrölä 2014). The makeover paradigm especially ties the fat body to consumer culture and the dutiful subject who is forever dieting, exercising, and beautifying herself to achieve the unattainable ideal body.

As my exploration of wellness for women showed in Chapter 5, women's body work is often presented in the guise of something that will make you both look and thus also feel better. Similarly, Gill notes that, in the media, women's body work is often portrayed as "fun" or as a form of "pampering", or as "taking time for oneself". Although body work takes a great deal of time and effort, this fact must somehow remain hidden and an air of naturalness and effortlessness should prevail (Gill 2007, p. 155). In this way, I would argue that postfeminist practices of self-governance and discipline become so ingrained in one's conduct that they become indiscernible from the self.

The neoliberal rationale behind the construction of femininity and female bodies in popular culture has been observed in women's magazines, television shows, and wider popular culture by a number of researchers (e.g. Gill 2007; 2008; Gonick 2006; Kauppinen 2012); while Dworkin and Wachs (2009, pp. 172–173) have particularly noted this in the context of fitness media.

Leslie Heywood, for her part, explores how the image of the female athlete has been harnessed to endorse neoliberalism. Heywood studied the promotion of sports programmes to girls and notes that the marketing of these programmes seems to unite feminism and neoliberalism by "presenting sport as a space where girls learn to become the ideal subjects of a new global economy that relies on individuals with flexibility who are trained to blame their inevitable failures on themselves rather than the system their lives are structured within" (Heywood 2007, p. 113). The fitness of the body becomes a code for equality that depends on the individual's effort.

> The image of the female athlete body does the cultural work of advertising equal opportunities – anyone can achieve this look if they just work hard enough (and anyone can succeed on all levels if they just work hard enough) – that masks the growing structural inequalities.
>
> (Heywood 2007, p. 117)

Heywood further notes that even if the moulding of the female body according to neoliberal rationale is not deliberate, the connection is inevitable due to the prevalence of these ideologies (2007, p. 117).

Abigail Saguy's observation, which I referred to in Chapter 1, resonates here. She suggests that feminist gender studies focus more on how medical research, public health campaigns, and news reports about fatness and the fat body affect women's physical image of themselves. Arguing that medical research, public health campaigns and news reports would not contribute to a "cult of thinness" in the age of healthism would be implausible at best; and again it illustrates the hegemony of biomedical discourse, and assumptions about its objectivity. Saguy is quick to point out that the aforementioned institutions are far from being objective in their approach to body size. There are, of course, cultural assumptions concerning body norms which also shape the production and reception of scientific knowledge (2013, p. 21).

Dworkin and Wachs, and Heywood seem to agree that the body's appearance and thinness is an important goal especially in women's fitness (Dworkin and Wachs 2009, pp. 172–173; Heywood 2007). They go on to argue that in fitness magazines which target women, the emphasis is more on thinness and toning the body (2009, pp. 172–173). They conclude that the notion of a fit and healthy subject in women's fitness magazines depends more on how the body looks than on actually being healthy. Women and men's bodies are also treated differently; while women's bodies are represented as objectified bodies, men seem to be able to transgress their bodies and occupy strong subject positions even while their bodies are being objectified.

It would seem that the requirement of "fitness" is, when referring to the body, yet another code for "thinness". The ideal female body is expected to be healthy and fit, but most importantly, these two criteria will also ensure thinness. Controlling body weight is, in itself, a way to discipline the female body, but demanding that the body looks fit at all times adds yet another level of control, and connects body control to neoliberal politics even more tightly, as fitness adds a moral element to a body that might already be thin anyway. In this respect, it would seem that neoliberal rationale has been either incorporated into feminist thinking concerning the female body and/or feminist thought is being appropriated by neoliberal culture.

Femininity for sale

The elements of postfeminist and neoliberal rationale that Gill listed are easily identifiable in the material world outside the media and in the present-day fat discourse that has been the focus of this book. Although the exact relationship between media culture and female subjectivity remains elusive, it would be hard to prove that there is no relationship between them (Gill 2008, p. 434). Media discourses reflect, rework, and reproduce our reality and we reflect, rework, and reproduce media discourses. Popular media is of course a thoroughly commercial field, which by virtue of this alone makes it an integral element of neoliberal culture. Popular media (especially that which is aimed at women) relies on the advertising revenue generated by the beauty, fashion, and dietary industries' marketing strategies.

For this reason alone, popular culture is a very important context for feminists. Driscoll explains feminists' interest in popular culture as interest in the ways modern life impacts women. Indeed, feminism itself is part of that popular culture. Feminism draws on popular culture and popular culture draws on feminism (Driscoll 1999, p. 173).

Even though we cannot be sure to what extent media discourses transfer into women's actual lives, we do know that the idea of marketing is to discover (and often to create) needs and desires, and for this purpose millions of euros are spent annually to manipulate consumer choice. The effectiveness of such manipulation can be measured in the number of sales. Women's "beauty work" is unavoidably connected to the logic of the market. Boundaries are increasingly confused in popular media, now that editorial material and adverts are often combined in what are called advertorials. It is obvious that certain types of commercialised and purchasable versions of femininity have an interest in promoting lifestyles that require attention to diet and exercise. Gill notes that to a much greater extent than men, women are required to work on and transform the self, regulate every aspect of their conduct, and present their actions as freely chosen. Could it be that neoliberalism is always already gendered, and that women are constructed as its ideal subjects (Gill 2007, p. 164)?

The answer, I would argue, seems to be yes. The relationship between capitalism, consumer culture, women, and women's bodies has been intimate all along (c.f. Bordo 1993; Featherstone 1991). Women *are* the people that spend the money on their own bodies, and so the beauty, fashion, and dietary industries almost exclusively rely on their willingness to spend time, effort, and money to work on their appearances. As part of this process, women are taught to consider their bodies as always somehow inadequate, always imperfect, and in constant need of work, products, treatments, rehabilitation, and surgery.

Women's ideals of beauty, body, and weight change however. This elusiveness of the perfect body or ideal weight makes them optimal consumers that can keep on consuming within their means endlessly. Women's bodies are part of the neo-liberal economy as products, and as consumers they have an incurable "illness", namely their female bodies. In a sense, women and men are both encouraged to think and treat women's bodies as property that women have to take care of, keep standard-sized, and ever youthful.

In the fat female body, the medicalisation of fatness and gendered norms and expectations of women's appearance meet. Medicalisation, where new illnesses to treat means more people will purchase more medicine; the commercial well-ness industry, where healthism and the moral imperative of health means more people will buy products and services to appear healthy; and the beauty industry, which requires women to achieve proper femininity, can be understood as part of the same continuum. As for the dietary industry, it is part of both the pharma-ceutical industry and beauty industry at the same time, and to some extent their interests are shared.

Postfeminist media construes self-management and self-discipline as part of female subjectivity, not as an external pressure. In postfeminist media dis-course, women are thus first and foremost responsible for producing themselves as desirable heterosexual subjects. This construction of heterosexual desirable femininity requires constant work, self-monitoring, discipline and emotional labour. In terms of postfeminist neoliberal rationale, women become entrepre-neurial subjects that perform femininity. One might however ask what is feminist about it? Kauppinen (2012, p. 96) comes to the conclusion, in her exploration of the language of *Cosmopolitan* magazine, that the discourse of postfeminist self-management that is so apparent in the magazine might appear feminist, but it operates according to the logic of neoliberal governmentality. Feminism is simply used as a means to create the entrepreneurial subject of neoliberalism. Kauppinen thinks that, for this reason, instead of feminism, we should be talking about gender-specific neoliberal governance. Similarly to Gill, Kauppinen says that women are the target subjects of neoliberal and women's magazines such as *Cosmopolitan*, and these are used to keep women mobilised in the task of becoming an entrepreneurial subject.

In the postfeminist era women's body norms remain the same or as strong as they ever were. What has changed is that they now seem to follow the logic of neoliberal governmentality. Women's body norms that were previously thought as something external, oppressive and imposed on women, now work through the internalisation of discipline and so-called "free" choice. Women become entre-preneurial subjects and in doing so, body work and performing femininity in a certain way become crucial.

Free choice and the thin privilege

As women's social success has always been more bound to appearance than men's, the social pressure to be thin is especially high for women (e.g. Bordo 1993, pp. 165–166). The requirement to self-monitor and discipline oneself and one's body is nothing new. In fact, these behaviours have been actively encouraged in girls' socialisation (Haug 1987) and schooling for decades and centuries (e.g. Lesko 1988; Harjunen 2002; Johannissen 1994).

In Western body culture, the acceptable size range of the female body has become very limited, moreover, fat phobia and fat hate are pronounced. It seems obvious that the free choice which forms the basis of neoliberal rationale does not therefore extend to body size. This fact limits many other choices too, namely all those other choices in life that might also lead to a size that is not socially acceptable for women. In terms of body size, those with the greatest free choice seem to already have the normative body, strive for it, and/or want the body to become "more normative". Since the body "project" must be realised in a limited manner and the result must be a normative-looking, normal sized or normatively performing female body, one can ask how much free choice there is after all. Moreover, by "choosing" a body/body shaping practice that does not comply with the norms, one inevitably places oneself outside the norm.

For women in particular, changing body size is only socially acceptable if the change results in a body that does not transgress the normative boundaries set for the size and shape of the female body. This applies both to women who work on the body "too much" or "too little". For example, female body builders who aim at developing a visibly muscular body (e.g. Haber 1996; Kinnunen 2001) and women engaging in extreme weight-loss and exercise practices such as women living with *anorexia nervosa* (Rich, Harjunen and Evans 2006) are considered to be taking the changes too far; while women who, judging from their appearance, do not engage in any kind of body-shaping practices or exercise that might result in weight loss are penalised for it by current healthist and neoliberal body culture in a number of ways. Another example of the strictness of the normative boundaries for female body size is how the benefits of weight loss are rarely questioned. Weight loss is approved and applauded even when women have lost weight due to a life-threatening illness. Active shaping of the body and appearance signals progress, goals, and a work ethic. Weight-loss dieting, as it is mostly performed by women, can be seen as part of the neoliberal performance of femininity.

Connected to the demand for women to conduct self-management invisibly is what Gill (2007, p. 152) observes as a shift in the objectification of the female body and subjectivity. Whereas women of yesteryear were represented as passive and objectified to please the assumed heterosexual male gaze, in present-day sexualised representations, women are portrayed as being active and in charge of choosing whether or not to objectify themselves. Objectification is no longer seen as oppressive or a result of the patriarchal male gaze, but as a freely chosen way to construct one's subjectivity. A willing objectification of one's own body is thus read as a sign of autonomy, empowerment, and sexual agency. What is crucial here is the shift from an external objectifying male gaze to the internalisation of a disciplinary regime. "In this regime, power is not imposed from above or from the outside, but constructs our very subjectivity" (Gill 2007, p. 152). Instead of engaging in body work because of external pressure and sexual objectification, women must now apparently do the body work just to be who they think they "really" are.

Although, it might seem so, the self that is being constructed here is not free from the male gaze. It is not a mere coincidence that the sexually liberated modern woman in media bears a strong resemblance to a heterosexual male fantasy (Gill 2007, p. 152). Postfeminist media products seem to celebrate female sexual agency, whilst also constructing it in a fashion that seems to offer freedom to please the male gaze. Troublingly, this is constructed as part of the female subjectivity, and yet again only a young, thin, and beautiful woman is seen as an active and liberated sexual subject.

Gill connects this representational shift to neoliberal subjectivity, which packages sexual objectification as something that women choose and want and is actually a sign of them being "active confident and assertive female subjects". "Freedom of choice" is central to postfeminist discourse, as it is to neoliberalism. In this case postfeminist discourse appears to suggest that equality has already been achieved and women can now act as autonomous agents free from the constraints of sexist power structures. Strangely enough though, all these freely choosing women, who apparently only want to please themselves, just happen to go for the same look. Freedom and autonomy are valued and assumed even when one is anything but. It is as if it is more important to appear to choose freely, while really all the time you are following a very normative idea of what the female body should look like.

As can be concluded from the bulk of critical scholarship in black studies, postcolonial studies, disability studies, lesbian and gay studies, queer studies, and fat studies, among others, the normative body of feminism has been an exclusive and tightly defined one. The assumed normative female subject has been white, middle class, heterosexual, Western, able-bodied and thin. Third-wave feminists have been more acutely aware of the diversity among women, and what that might mean for their experience of the world as embodied subjects. Women's intersectional differences resulting from sexuality, class, race, and abilities have thus featured strongly in both academic and popular feminist discussion from the 1990s onwards. Third-wave feminists recognise that there is no one particular defining universal female experience that feminism can draw on; it is against this backdrop that questions concerning female subjectivity, agency and the body are played out today in feminist scholarship.

In the 2000s conscious attempts to subvert and diversify body norms, by extending, reworking, or "queering" them (e.g. Pausé, Wykes and Murray 2014) in some way have become more frequent. This has been identified, for example, in women's body modification practices such as tattooing (e.g. Mifflin 1997), and in efforts to reclaim the fat female body from the sphere of medical determination and relocate it to the sphere of the cultural and social (e.g. LeBesco 2004). Examples of the latter are, for instance, the phenomenon of "fatshion" that has spread through blogs that concentrate on fashion for fat people (e.g. Tovar 2012);

talking about and theorising fat sex and sexuality (e.g. Blank 2015; Hester and Walters 2015); and the wider movements of body positivity and body diversity, the motto of which could be "every body is a good body", which have spread across the internet and social media. Attempting to change the general perception of bodies that have been previously condemned as non-normative, stigmatised, or undesirable forms of femininity can be seen as a means to resist hegemony, as well as a method to empower its embodied subjects. However, the fact that many of these changes towards a more diverse and more inclusive body culture have taken place through and with the help of neoliberal capitalism cannot be overlooked and needs to be taken into account. Neither can it be ignored that a "liberation" which requires financial assets will always be out of reach of some groups of women, most likely the ones who would need it the most.

8   Conclusion

In the beginning of this book, I set myself two main goals: to look into the ways by which, in contemporary Western culture, the gendered fat body becomes (and is made) intelligible in the context of "neoliberal culture"; and to explore how neoliberal rationale takes part in moulding acceptable and unacceptable gendered bodies – in terms of what is healthy and unhealthy. My intention was to cultivate the idea that the emergence of fatness as a global phenomenon in the late 1990s and early 2000s, is connected to neoliberal culture and is part of the construction I have called the "neoliberal body".

I have proposed that neoliberal rationale plays an important part in the formation of present-day body culture and aimed to show that today's body culture comprises a number of policies, discourses, and practices that can be perceived in terms of economic and neoliberal governmentality. I have concentrated here on how neoliberal governmentality, in its many forms, affects the fat body and contributes to its vilification. I have focused on policies, discourses, and practices that are designed to eliminate fatness or that contribute to that purpose in some way, such as the medicalisation of fatness and the obesity epidemic discourse; the economisation of health and healthcare; healthism; and postfeminism. I have, for example, suggested that the obesity epidemic discourse is part of a broader neoliberal culture of health and a part of the neoliberal governance of bodies.

I have shown that the way fatness and the fat body are approached is influenced by ideology, particularly the neoliberal rationale that permeates present-day Western culture. In neoliberal culture the fat body is not just the unhealthy body one finds in medical discourse, but also the body that is costly, unproductive, and inefficient, which is failing in the crucial task of self-management. My intention has not been to prove that the construction of the neoliberal body is a systematic or a seamless "project", and yet it should not be considered a haphazard development either. Neoliberal economic policy has permeated society in various forms and structures, from institutions to individual bodies. Neoliberalism as governmentality binds together many discourses and practices concerning the body, while also generating new connections between them, and thus tightening their relationship. These discourses can be identified separately, but they can also be seen as part of a larger whole, and among other things, they are always gendered and classed.

It seems evident that the neoliberal body is being constructed in a number of connected spheres at the same time. Regarding the fat body, neoliberal governmentality seems to fuse the interests of a number of actors in, for example, public policy, the market, the patriarchy, and the individual. The medicalisation and stigmatisation of fat bodies via the obesity epidemic discourse certainly benefits the market, but it also acts as a vehicle for neoliberal biopolitical governance, as the commercialisation of health services increases the need for the population to self-manage these aspects of their life.

Indeed, the notion of fatness and the fat body as something diseased, costly, immoral, ugly, and above all, a symbol of individual failure, would probably not have such an impact were it not produced and maintained, at the same time, in so many spheres – discursive and otherwise. This is the power of neoliberal governmentality. The fat body, or perhaps in this case the pathologised obese body, seems to be a particularly susceptible target for the different modes of neoliberal governmentality that I have presented in this book.

The preferred body of neoliberalism

In their work on cultural cloning Essed and Goldberg (2002) suggest that a "preferred type" is being actively produced in society. Their main interest is how gendered and racialised likeness is reproduced. Cultural cloning is about producing a likeness, but not only in the sense of imitation. The likeness in bodies that is reproduced is the normative and privileged body. Producing the preferred type is about power dynamics, specifically those that concern the division of status and privilege within society. Production of certain types of bodies by or with the help of neoliberal governmentality could perhaps be seen as one variation of culturally cloning the preferred type that Essed and Goldberg discuss. There definitely seems to be a "preferred" body that is being reproduced in neoliberal culture, which is one that seems to embody its core values.

In the introduction I asked whether there is a preferred neoliberal body and tentatively suggested that the fat body could perhaps be considered as *the* neoliberal body. This might seem a bit strange now, after all that has been described in this book. Surely neoliberal bodies are those which are lean and mean, high achieving, superbly performing, self-reliant, responsible, self-managing and entrepreneurial bodies? The archetypical example of this type of body would be the long-distance running, triathlon-competing, fitness-training, health-conscious citizen that the media so often offers up as the embodiment of our times. Indeed, most of the time the representation of this body is of an upper-middle class white male. However, the bodies neoliberal culture produces through discourses and discursive practice are not just the preferred ones. When talking about neoliberal body culture, there is more at stake than just identifying the qualities of "Ms. or Mr. Neoliberal Ideal Body". What about those bodies that neoliberal culture apparently rejects? Construction of a cultural norm also implies constructing the "other" that it would like to exclude, and yet which is just as much a product of that culture. It is enticing to think about stigmatisation and attempts to eradicate fatness as the flipside of sameness or going for the preferred body type. After all, unequal power relationships must surely be constructed through the cultural preference for sameness, just as they are in the cultural aversion towards those who are marked out as different or troublesome.

So if the ideal neoliberal body is the one that seems to embody and represent those values most often associated with neoliberal economic policy such as productivity, efficiency, cost-productiveness, control, self-reliance, and high performance, the "other" body of neoliberal (body) culture (among other rejected bodies) is one that is assumed to represent people that are unproductive, risky, dependent, and lacking responsibility in society. As noted earlier, it does not seem a mere coincidence that the fat body has become the most reviled body of the neoliberal era. Stereotypes and prejudices concerning fatness and the fat body have certainly existed since long before this era (e.g. Farrell 2011), but there is no denying that disapproval of fatness seems to fit particularly well into the neoliberal agenda. Women take the main brunt of the fat stigma, but it is not just about fat female bodies. This "policing of the body" is intense for all. Public surveillance, monitoring and evaluation of the body have only intensified in the era of social media. The public shaming of women's bodies is an everyday occurrence and there is no escaping this judgemental gaze; if anything, certain postfeminist ideas concerning the female body ironically seem to play along with it too.

I have aimed to show that the norm of thinness is perpetuated by neoliberal body culture and that it places fat people in the role of a necessary "other" which simultaneously allows thin people to be placed in a privileged position. Thinness brings with it social and cultural benefits that people with other body sizes do not enjoy. The thin norm as a category of privilege can be seen as parallel and intersecting with the male norm, the white norm, and the middle-class and able-bodied norm; it certainly intersects with all of them.

The thin norm and thin privilege are supported particularly by medical, healthist and economic discourses that draw from neoliberalism; however, it should be noted that the range of acceptable thinness is also limited. Those too fat or too thin are positioned as "marginal" or "pathological" identities and they are both considered in need of restoration. It seems that when body size is very strictly determined in this way, those bodies that deviate from the norm become easily labelled as faulty or abnormal (Rich, Harjunen and Evans 2006).

The obesity epidemic discourse can be seen as a part of neoliberal culture and a neoliberal mode of governing of bodies, which aims at producing a certain type of embodied subject. It exemplifies how the "other" body in neoliberal culture is constructed too. There is an unnecessary dualism and division in neoliberal body culture with a pronounced sense of what makes a body good, and what makes it bad determined simply by neoliberal rationale. Present-day discussions on health, for example, rely on the idea that a neoliberal subject will always make or at least want to make rational (i.e. good) choices regarding health, when clearly these decisions are never that simple. Those who seem to be failing are nevertheless morally scorned and socially punished, and the obesity epidemic discourse has been instrumental in this.

Neoliberal rationale is based on the twin pillars of freedom and choice, and healthism is an extension of this construction so that it also covers health and well-being. However, making choices about health clearly does not just depend on an individual's own free will. There are structural, socioeconomic, cultural and other factors which play a significant role and are beyond most individuals' control. The playing field on which to make these "free" choices is thus far from level. Neoliberal body culture, however, would have us ignore these "levels" of freedom and see them instead as "moral differences". With its emphasis on individual choice, it thus enhances the inequalities resulting from wrong or irrational choices instead. The demands to self-manage and govern the body that are typical of neoliberal governmentality especially target women. This means that the penalties for apparently failing to do so are harder for them.

Here I come back to Essed and Goldberg's (2002, p. 1069) notion of cloning cultures mentioned in the introduction. They have noted that those who fall out of the "preferred type" are in danger of becoming dehumanised; and episodes of moral panic such as those promoted by the obesity epidemic discourse will do just that to a group of people, i.e. their worth as human beings is denied and they are considered as somehow inferior. Dehumanisation is definitely one of the serious negative side effects of moral panic, as when a group of people is stigmatised as morally inferior, deviant, and thus as less human in some way, this only furthers greater discrimination, and so the situation worsens. One dangerous consequence of this is that ever more radical ways of solving the problem appear and are regarded as justifiable, even though they may not be, and might actually be regarded by others as, unfair and harmful. Moral panic thus shifts the boundaries of what is considered the morally justifiable treatment of other people.

How we think about, treat, and feel about fatness and the fat body in neoliberal culture raises some important questions about contemporary body culture and how we govern our bodies in general. It is obviously *not* just the fat body that is seen as wasteful and expensive in neoliberal culture. The poor, the old, the disabled, and the chronically ill, for example, are all perceived through the neoliberal lens as having bodies that will be a cost and burden to our society. The neoliberal body is thus in fact highly exclusive and individualised, and becoming one is not an option that is available for everyone, no matter how well they might self-manage and govern themselves. Besides, neoliberal individuals are not supposed to become *too* self-reliant or independent, otherwise they would no longer need the market that is seen to be so vital for everything; it is only "freedom from the state" that is being advocated. It seems the only way the excessive and the wasteful can become proper neoliberal subjects is through private consumerism and to engage wholeheartedly in the process of becoming better, improved, and more effective versions of ourselves. In this task, the market is always ready to help. However, one needs stay alert when consuming, since there is a moral catch involved. As Guthman and DuPuis (2006, p. 445) say, in the era of excess, those who want less are revered. They point out the paradox, however, that simply wanting less is not enough though; "the neoliberal citizen is charged with wanting less but at the same time spending more".

Some final words

One of the inspirations for writing this book was the observation that discussions on fatness (but also on health, fitness, and nutrition) were becoming increasingly hot topics. In the process of writing this book, I have also become more conscious both of body culture and healthism (in the Crawfordian sense). They seem to have achieved momentum in Finland over the past five to ten years, judging from discussions concerning health and fitness which seem to be permeated with healthism's particular brand of neoliberal governmentality.

Fatness has been the constant focus of public discussion since the early 2000s when the obesity epidemic discourse hit the mainstream media (cf. Kyrölä 2007). This obesity panic has been followed by a public debate on nutrition and diet that was at its most heated in 2010–2013. Official dietary guidelines have been challenged to the extent that during the most intense period of the debate, the health authorities responsible for designing official dietary guidelines received hate mail – even death threats (e.g. Fogelholm 2012). At the same time there has been a potent wellness and fitness boom: long-distance running, CrossFit training, body fitness, and gym training have risen in popularity and have become practically mandatory occupations for many. Professions such as "personal trainer" and "life coach" have also become more widespread and available to a wider public. Tellingly, in the space of few years, having one's own personal trainer is no longer a luxury affordable only to the more affluent gym-goer. Gyms have their own dieting groups, and the range of private wellness and health products and services has expanded. A wide variety of services marketed under this notion of "wellness" such as mindfulness, meditation, and so on, have also become widely available. All of this has caught my attention and continues to fascinate me.

It intrigues me, for instance, how certain body practices are now marketed for women as a means to empowerment while at the same time women's body ideals remain exactly the same and the body norms regarding size and weight are as strict as ever. "Doing health" for women has become yet another code for beauty and beauty work (cf. Dworkin and Wachs 2009), not to mention a mode of control. In fact, it could be claimed that postfeminism as a means of contemporary feminist sensibility (e.g. Gill 2007) seems to enforce both internalised and external "body policing" on women, rather than relieve them of it.

As Crawford (2006) observes, the middle classes are both the primary agent and primary target of healthism. On a speculative note, I am inclined to think that the overall neoliberalisation of society can be seen in the adopted body practices of certain middle classes and the way these practices are used to distinguish themselves from lower socioeconomic classes. The preoccupation and willingness to work on one's body might express an unvoiced wish that it will somehow ensure one's survival in an ever more forbidding society where income inequalities are growing, welfare state safety nets are being actively dismantled, and the labour market is increasingly competitive. Neoliberal body culture seems to prepare the middle classes for a battle, which might not be so much about the health and fitness of individuals, but is definitely about control and power: who controls these individuals and their bodies, and for what purpose.

In a culture where neoliberal governmentality reigns, there is no need to coerce or discipline people, because people discipline themselves voluntarily. While people make it their duty to become a self-governing subject, the act of doing so is often misinterpreted as a sign of superior morals and deservingness. In this way, this class of people not only differentiates itself from the "others", but also helps to dismiss them as being somehow in the "wrong" too. Whether it is an unwillingness or inability to become self-controlled and have a disciplined body in the ways that are deemed appropriate, it nevertheless becomes socially unacceptable and immoral both in reference to personal morals and one's role in society. As individual body management and economic success within society become conflated, success in body management becomes the sign of a well-adjusted neoliberal citizen who has taken responsibility over their health and therefore society. Fatness then is interpreted not just a sign of an individual's immorality, but also of not being a proper neoliberal subject.

References

Aarva, P. and Lääperi, P. 2005. Terveysretoriikka pääkirjoituksissa. Helsingin Sanomien ja Aamulehden välittämä kuva terveyden edistämisestä vuosina 2002–2003. *Duodecim* 121, pp. 71–78.

Aphramor, L. and Gingras, J. R., 2008. Sustaining imbalance: evidence of neglect in the pursuit of nutritional health. In: Riley, S., Burns, M., Frith, H., Wiggins, S., and Markula, P., eds. *Critical bodies: representations, practices and identities of weight and body management*. London: Palgrave, pp. 155–174.

Ayo, N., 2012. Understanding health promotion in a neoliberal climate and the making of health conscious citizens. *Critical Public Health*, 22 (1), pp. 99–105.

Bartky, S., 1990. *Femininity and domination: studies in the phenomenology of oppression*. New York: Routledge.

Beauvoir de, S., 2011 [1949]. *The second sex*. New York: Vintage.

Berg, P., 2010. *Ryhmärajoja ja hierarkioita: etnografinen tutkimus peruskoulun yläasteen liikunnanopetuksesta*. E-thesis [online] Helsingin yliopisto. Available at: http://urn.fi/URN:ISBN:978-952-10-5995-7 [Accessed 22 March 2016].

Biltekoff, C., 2007. The terror within: obesity in the post 9/11 U.S. life. *American Studies*, 48 (3), pp. 29–48.

Blank, H., 2015. *Big big love: a sourcebook on sex for people of size and those who love them*. Eugene, OR: Greenery Press.

Boero, N., 2012. *Killer fat: media, medicine and morals in the American obesity epidemic*. New Brunswick, NJ: Rutgers University Press.

Bordo, S.,1993. *Unbearable weight: feminism, Western culture and the body*. Berkeley, CA: University of California Press.

Braziel Evans, J., and LeBesco, K., 2001. *Bodies out of bounds: fatness and transgression*. Berkeley, CA: University of California Press.

Brink, P. J., 1994. Stigma and obesity. *Clinical Nursing Research*, 34, pp. 291–293.

Broom, D., 2008. Hazardous good intentions? Unintended consequences of the project of prevention. *Health Sociology Review*, 17 (2), pp. 129–140.

Brown, W., 2003. Neo-liberalism and the end of liberal democracy. *Theory & Event*, 7 (1) [online] Available at: https://muse.jhu.edu/journals/theory_and_event/v007/7.1brown.html [Accessed 22 March 2016].

Brownell, K., and Teachman, B., 2000. Implicit anti-bias among health professionals: is anyone immune? *International Journal of Obesity*, 25, pp. 1525–1531.

Caballero, B., 2007. The global epidemic of obesity: an overview. *Epidemiological Review*, 29, pp. 1–5.

Campos, P., 2004. *The obesity myth: why America's obsession with weight is hazardous to your health*. New York: Gotham.

Campos, P., Saguy, A., Ernsberger, P., Oliver, E. and Gaesser, G., 2006. The epidemiology of overweight and obesity: public health crisis or moral panic? *International Journal of Epidemiology*, 35, pp. 55–60.

Cao, S., Moineddin, R., Urquia, M. L., Razak, F., and Ray, J. G., 2014. J-shapedness: an often missed, often miscalculated relation: the example of weight and mortality. *Journal of Epidemiological Community Health*, 68, pp. 683–690.

Cederström, C., and Spicer, A., 2015. *The wellness syndrome*. Cambridge: Polity Press.

Cheek, J., 2008. Healthism: a new conservatism? *Qualitative Health Research*, 18 (7), pp. 974–982.

Chernin, K., 1981.*The obsession: reflections on the tyranny of slenderness*. New York: Harper & Row.

Cogan, J. C., 1999. Re-evaluating the weight-centred approach toward health. In: Sobal, J. and Maurer, D. eds. *Interpreting weight: The social management of fatness and thinness*. New York: Aldine de Gruyter, pp. 229–253.

Cohen, S., 1972. *Folk devils and moral panics*. London: McGibbon & Kee.

Conrad, P., 2007. *The medicalization of society: on the transformation of human conditions into treatable disorders*. Baltimore, MD: Johns Hopkins University Press.

Cooper, C., 1997. Can a fat woman call herself disabled? *Disability & Society*, 12 (1), pp. 31–41.

Cooper, C., 1998. *Fat and proud: the politics of size*. London: Women's Press.

Cooper, C., 2010. Fat studies: mapping the field. *Sociology Compass*, 4 (12), pp. 1020–1034.

Crawford, R., 1980. Healthism and the medicalization of everyday life. *International Journal of Health Services*, 10 (3), pp. 365–388.

Crawford, R., 2006. Health as a meaningful social practice. *Health: An Interdisciplinary Journal for the Social Study of Health, Illness and Medicine*, 10 (4), pp. 401–420.

Critser, G., 2004. *Fat land: how Americans became the fattest people in the world*. New York, NY: Houghton Mifflin.

Curtis, J. P., Selter, J. G., Wand, Y., Rathore, S. S., Jovin, I. S., Jadbabaie, F., Kosiboror, M., Portnay, E. L., Sokol, S. I., Bader, F., and Krumholz, H. M., 2005. The obesity paradox: body mass index and outcomes in patients with heart failure. *Arch Intern Med.*, 165 (1), pp. 55–61.

Dahlgren, J., 2008. Neoliberal reforms in Swedish primary health care: for whom and for what purpose? *International Journal of Health Services*, 38, pp. 697–715.

Davis, K., 1995. *Reshaping the female body: the dilemma of cosmetic surgery*. New York: Routledge.

Davis, K., 2008. Intersectionality as buzzword: a sociology of science perspective on what makes a feminist theory successful. *Feminist Theory*, 9 (1), pp. 167–185.

Driscoll, C., 1999. Girl culture, revenge and global capitalism: cybergirls, riot grrls, Spice Girls. *Australian Feminist Studies*, 14 (29), pp. 173–193.

Dworkin, S., and Wachs, F., 2009. *Body panic: gender, health, and the selling of fitness*. NYC: New York University Press.

Elonin, P., 2014. Hallitus kirii maaliin myöhässä – vyön kiristys jatkuu vuosia.Valtiontalous on kohtuullisessa kunnossa vasta vuonna 2018. *Helsingin Sanomat* (HS), 4 April. [online] Available at: http://www.hs.fi/kotimaa/a1396500353905 [Accessed 22 March 2016].

Erola, J., 2009. Sosiaalisen aseman periytyvyys ja terveys – tulokset, teoriat ja tulevaisuus. *Sosiaalilääketieteellinen Aikakauslehti*, 46 (1), pp. 3–13.

Eräsaari, L., 2002. *Julkinen tila ja valtion yhtiöittäminen*. Helsinki: Gaudeamus.

Essed, P. 2005. Gendered preferences in racialized spaces: cloning the physician. In: Murji, K. and Solomos, J. eds. *Racialization: studies in theory and practice*. Oxford: Oxford University Press, pp. 227–248.

Essed, P., and Goldberg, D. T., 2002. Cloning cultures: the social injustices of sameness. *Ethnic and Racial Studies*, 25 (6), pp. 1066–1082.

Farrell, A. E., 2011. *Fat shame: stigma and the fat body in American culture*. New York: NYU Press.

Faubion, J. D. ed., 1994. *Four essential works of Foucault 1954–1984*. London: Penguin Books.

Featherstone, M., 1991 [1982]. The body in consumer culture. In: Featherstone, M., Hepworth, M. and Turner, B. S., eds. *The body: social process and cultural theory*. London: Sage, pp. 170–196.

Fitzgerald, F. T., 1994. The tyranny of health. *The New England Journal of Medicine*, 331, pp. 196–198.

Flegal, K. M., Graubard, B. I., Williamson, D. F., and Gail M. H., 2005. Excess death associated with underweight, overweight and obesity. *Journal of the American Medical Association*, Apr 20, 293 (15), pp. 1861–1867.

Flegal, K. M., Graubard, B., Williamson, D.F., and Gail, M. H., 2007. Impact of smoking and pre-existing illness on estimates of the fractions of deaths associated with underweight, overweight, and obesity in the US population. *American Journal of Epidemiology*, 1668, pp. 975–982.

Flegal, K. M., Kit, B. K., Orpana, H., and Graubard, B. I., 2013. Association of all-cause mortality with overweight and obesity using standard body mass index categories: a systematic review and meta-analysis. *Journal of the American Medical Association*, 309 (1), pp. 71–82.

Fogelholm, M., 2012. Ravitsemustutkijat kovilla julkisessa keskustelussa. *Tieteessä tapahtuu*, 30 (1), pp. 1–2.

Fonarow, G. C., Srikanthan, P., Costanzo, M. R., Cintron, G. B., Lopatin, M., ADHERE Scientific Advisory Committee and Investigators, 2007. An obesity paradox in acute heart failure: analysis of body mass index and in hospital mortality for 108,927 patients in the acute decompensated Heart Failure National Registry, *American Heart Journal*, 153 (1), pp. 74–81.

Foucault, M., 1979. *Discipline and punish*. Harmondsworth: Penguin.

Foucault, M., 1990. *The history of sexuality. Vol.1: the will to knowledge*. London: Penguin.

Foucault, M., 1991 [1978]. Governmentality (Lecture at the Collège de France, 1 Feb. 1978). In: Burchell, G., Gordon, C., and Miller, P. eds., *The Foucault effect: studies in Governmentality*. Hemel Hempstead: Harvester Wheatsheaf, pp. 87–104.

Gailey, J., 2014. *The hyper(in)visible fat woman*. New York: Palgrave Macmillan.

Gard, M., and Wright, J., 2005. *The obesity epidemic: science, morality and ideology*. New York: Routledge.

Gennep, van, A. 1960 [1909]. *Rites of passage*. Chicago: University of Chicago Press.

Gerber, L., 2011. *Seeking the straight and narrow: weight loss and sexual reorientation in evangelical America*. Chicago: The University of Chicago Press.

Gerhard, J., 2005. Carrie Bradshaw's queer postfeminism. *Feminist Media Studies*, 5 (1), pp. 38–49.

Gill, R., 2007. Postfeminist media culture: elements of a sensibility. *European Journal of Cultural Studies*, 10 (147), pp. 147–166.

Gill, R., 2008. Culture and subjectivity in neoliberal and postfeminist times. *Subjectivity*, 25, pp. 432–445.

Glassner, B., 1999. *The culture of fear*. New York: Basic Books.

Goffman, E., 1963. *Stigma: notes on the management of spoiled identity*. Harmondsworth: Penguin.

Gonick, M., 2006. Between "girl power" and "Reviving Ophelia": constituting the neoliberal girl subject. *NWSA Journal*, 18 (2), pp. 1–23.

Goode, E. and Ben-Yehuda N., 1994. *Moral panics: the social construction of deviance.* Oxford, UK and Cambridge, MA: Blackwell, pp. 57–65.

Goold, I., Skene, L., Herring, J., and Greasley, K., 2014. The concise argument: the human body as property? Possession, control and commodification. *J Med Ethics*,40, pp. 1–2. [online] Available at: http://jme.bmj.com/content/40/1/1.full [Accessed 22 March 2016].

Grabowski, D. C., and Ellis, J. E., 2001. High body mass index does not predict mortality in older people: analysis of the longitudinal study of aging. *Journal of American Geriatric Society*, 497 (Jul), pp. 968–79.

Guthman, J., 2009. Teaching the politics of obesity: insights into neoliberal embodiment and contemporary biopolitics. *Antipode*, 41 (5), pp. 1110–1133.

Guthman, J., 2011. *Weighing in: obesity, food justice, and the limits of capitalism*. Berkeley, CA: University of California Press.

Guthman, J., and DuPuis, M., 2006. Embodying neoliberalism: economy, culture, and the politics of fat. *Environment and Planning: Society and Space*, 24, pp. 427–448.

Haber, H. F., 1996. Foucault pumped: body politics and the muscled woman. In: Hekman, S., ed. *Feminist interpretation of Michel Foucault*. Pennsylvania: The Pennsylvania State University Press, pp. 137–156.

Hänninen, S., and Sarlio-Lähteenkorva, S., 2005. Naisen ideaalivartalo laihdutustuotemainonnassa ja vaikeasti lihavien laihduttajanaisten puheessa. *Naistutkimus–Kvinnoforskning*, 18 (3), pp. 30–40.

Harjunen, H., 2002. The construction of the acceptable female body in Finnish school. In: Sunnari, V., Kangasvuo, J. and Heikkinen, M. eds., *Gendered and sexualized violence in educational environments*. Femina Borealis publication series no 5. Oulu: Oulu University Press.

Harjunen, H., 2004a. Exploring obesity through the social model of disability. In: Kristiansen, K., and Traustadóttir, R. eds., *Gender and disability research in the Nordic countries*. Lund: Studentlitteratur.

Harjunen, H., 2004b. Lihavuus ja moraalinen paniikki. *Yhteiskuntapolitiikka*, 2, pp. 412–418.

Harjunen, H., 2006. Liikaa tai ei lainkaan: käsityksiä lihavan naisen seksuaalisuudesta. In: Puuronen, A. and Kinnunen, T. eds., *Seksuaalinen ruumis*. Helsinki: Gaudeamus, pp. 183–197.

Harjunen, H., 2009. *Women and fat: approaches to the social study of fatness*. Jyväskylä Studies in Education, Psychology and Social Research no 379. Jyväskylä: The University of Jyväskylä.

Harjunen, H., 2012. Lihavuus yhteiskunnallisena kysymyksenä. In: Harjunen, H. and Saresma, T. eds., *Sukupuoli nyt. Purkamisia ja neuvotteluja*. Jyvaskyla: Kampus Kustannus.

Harjunen, H., and Kyrölä, K., 2007. Lihavuustutkimusta toisin. In: Kyrölä, K. and Harjunen, H. eds. *Koolla on väliä: koon, ruumisnormien ja lihavuuden politiikat*. Helsinki: Like. pp. 9–46.

Härkönen, J., and Räsänen, P., 2008. Liikalihavuus, työttömyys ja ansiotaso. *Työelämäntutkimus – Arbetslivsforskning*, 6 (1), pp. 3–16.

Harrison, E., 2012. The body economic: the case of 'childhood obesity'. *Feminism & Psychology*, 22 (3), pp. 324–343.

Harvey, D., 2007. *A brief history of neoliberalism*. Oxford: Oxford University Press.

Haug, F. ed., 1987. *Female sexualization: a collective work of memory*. London: Verso.

Heiskanen, R., 2009. Lahjoittaja ostaa ihmisläskiä 15€/kilo. *Ilta-sanomat*, 29 November [online] Available at: http://www.iltalehti.fi/laihdutus/2009122910852678_lh.shtml [Accessed 22 March 2016].

Helén, I., and Jauho, J., 2003. Terveyskansalaisuus ja elämänpolitiikka. In Helén, I. and Jauho, M. eds., *Kansalaisuus ja kansanterveys*. Helsinki: Gaudeamus, pp. 13–32.

Heliövaara, M., and Aromaa, A.,1980. *Suomalaisten aikuisten pituus, paino ja lihavuus.* 19, Kansaneläkelaitoksen julkaisuja. Kansaneläkelaitoksen autoklinikka ja sosiaaliturvan tutkimuslaitos.

Henriksson, L., and Wrede, S., 2008. Care work in the context of transforming welfare state. In Wrede S., et al., eds., *Care work in crisis: reclaiming the Nordic ethos of care.* Lund: Studentlitteratur, pp. 121–130.

Herndon, A., 2005. Collateral damage from friendly fire?: race, nation, class, and the "war against obesity". *Social Semiotics*, 15 (82), pp. 127–141.

Hesse-Biber, S., 1996. Am I thin enough yet?: the cult of thinness and the commercialization of identity. Oxford: Oxford University Press.

Hester, H. and Walters. C., 2015. *Fat sex: new directions in theory and activism.* Farnham, UK: Ashgate.

Heyes, C. J., 2006. Foucault goes to Weight Watchers. *Hypatia*, 21 (2), pp. 126–148.

Heywood, V. 1996. *Dedication to hunger: the anorexic aesthetic in modern culture.* Berkeley, CA: University of California Press.

Heywood, L., 2007. Producing girls: empire, sport, and the neoliberal body. In: Hargreaves, J., and Vertinsky, P. eds. *Physical culture, power, and the body.* New York: Routledge, pp. 101–120.

Hirvonen, H., 2014. *Habitus and care: investigating health care workers agency.* Jyväskylä Studies in Education, Psychology and Social Research 497. Jyväskylä: The University of Jyväskylä.

Hofmann, B., 2015. Obesity as a socially defined disease: philosophical considerations and implications for policy and care. *Health Care Analysis* [online] Available at: http://www.ncbi.nlm.nih.gov/pubmed/25822670 [Accessed 22 March 2016].

Hölttä, K., 2013. Puheenaihe: Komissaari Rehn uskoo yhä talouskuriin. *Aamulehti*, 19 July [online]. Available at: http://www.aamulehti.fi/juttuarkisto/?cid=1194827113902 [Accessed 22 March 2016].

Huff, J., 2001. A horror of corpulence: interrogating bantingism and mid-nineteenth-century fat-phobia. In Braziel Evans, J., and LeBesco, K. eds., *Bodies out of bounds: fatness and transgression*. Berkeley: University of California Press, pp. 39–59.

Hukkanen, V., 2005. Esko Aho korottaisi hoitomaksuja kuntonsa laiminlyöjiltä. *Kauppalehti*, 31 August, p. 2.

Hynynen, E-L., 2010. Kahden terveydenhuollon maa. *Suomen Kuvalehti*, 21, pp. 26–32.

Johannissen, K., 1994. *Den mörka kontinenten.* Stockholm: Norstedts.

Julkunen, R., 2004. Hyvinvointipalvelujen uusi politiikka. In: Henriksson, L. and Wrede, S. eds., *Hyvinvointityön ammatit*. Helsinki: Gaudeamus, pp. 168–188.

Kalantar-Zadeh, K., *et al.*, 2003. Reverse epidemiology of cardiovascular risk factors in maintenance dialysis patients. *Kidney International*, 63, pp. 793–808.

Kalantar-Zadeh, K., *et al.*, 2007. Racial and survival paradoxes in chronic kidney disease. *Nature Clinical Practice Nephrology*, 3, pp. 493–506.

Kassirer, J. P., and Angell, M., 1998. Losing weight: an ill-fated New Year's resolution. *The New England Journal of Medicine*, 3381, pp. 52–54.

Kauppinen, K., 2012. At an intersection of postfeminism and neoliberalism: a discourse analytical view of an international women's magazine. *Critical Approaches to Discourse Analysis Across Disciplines*, 7 (1), pp. 82–99.

Kauppinen, K., and Anttila, E., 2005. Onko painolla väliä: hoikat, lihavat ja normaalipainoiset naiset työelämän murroksessa? *Työ ja perhe aikakauskirja 2, Työ, perhe ja elämän moninaisuus II.* Työterveyslaitoksen julkaisuja.

Käyhkö, M., 2006. *Siivoojaksi oppimassa. Etnografinen tutkimus työläistytöistä puhdistuspalvelualan koulutuksessa.* Joensuu: Joensuu University Press.

Kettunen, P., 2001. The Nordic welfare state in Finland. *Scandinavian Journal of History*, 26 (3), pp. 225–247.

Kinnunen, T., 2001. *Pyhät bodarit: yhteisöllisyys ja onni täydellisessä ruumiissa.* Helsinki: Gaudeamus.

Kinnunen, T., 2008. *Lihaan leikattu kauneus.* Helsinki: Gaudeamus.

Kirkland, A., 2014. Wellness as buzzword. *Journal of Health Politics, Policy and Law*, 39 (5), pp. 957–970.

Kosonen, U., 1998. *Koulumuistoja naiseksi kasvamisesta.* Jyväskylä: SoPhi.

Kullgren, J. T., Troxel, A. B., Loewenstein, G., Asch, D. A., Norton, L. A., Wesby, L., Tao, Y., Zhu, J., and Volpp, K. G., 2013. Individual- versus group-based financial incentives for weight loss: a randomized, controlled trial. *Annals of Internal Medicine*, 158 (7), pp. 505–14.

Kuusi, P., 1961. *60-luvun sosiaalipolitiikka.* Helsinki: WSOY.

Kyrölä, K., 2007. Lihavuusvaara! pelon politiikka ja lihava ruumiillisuus Helsingin sanomissa. In: Kyrölä, K. and Harjunen, H. eds. *Koolla on väliä: lihavuus, ruumisnormit ja sukupuoli.* Helsinki: Like, pp. 49–82.

Kyrölä, K., 2014. *The weight of images: affect, body image and fat in the media.* Farnham: Ashgate.

LeBesco, K., 2004. *Revolting bodies: the struggle to redefine fat identity.* Amherst & Boston: University of Massachusetts Press.

LeBesco, K., 2007. Fatness as the embodiment of working class rhetoric. In: DeGenero, W., ed. *Who says? Working-class rhetoric, class consciousness, and community.* Pittsburgh, PA: University of Pittsburgh Press, pp. 238–255.

LeBesco, K., 2010. Fat panic and the new morality. In: Metzl, J. and Kirkland, A., eds. *Against health: how health became the new morality.* New York: New York University Press, pp. 72–82.

LeBesco, K., 2011. Neoliberalism, public health and the moral perils of fatness. *Critical Public Health*, 21 (2), pp. 153–164.

Lee, C. D., Blair, S. N., and Jackson A. S., 1999. Cardiorespiratory fitness, body composition, and all-cause and cardiovascular disease mortality in men. *The American Journal of Clinical Nutrition*, 69 (3), pp. 373–80.

Lemke, T., 2001. The birth of bio-politics – Michel Foucault's lecture at the Collège de France on neo-liberal governmentality. *Economy and Society*, 30 (2), pp. 1–17.

Lesko, N., 1988. The curriculum of the body: lessons from Catholic high school. In: Roman, L. G., Christian-Smith, L. K, and Ellsworth, E. A., eds. *Becoming feminine: the politics of popular culture.* Basingstoke: Falmer Press, pp. 123–142.

Louderback, L., 1970. *Fat power: whatever you weigh is right.* Portland, OR: Hawthorn Books.

Lupton, D., 1995. *The imperative of health: public health and the regulated body.* London: Sage.

MacSween, M., 1993. *Anorexic bodies: a feminist and sociological perspective on Anorexia Nervosa.* London: Routledge.

Mäkelä, J., and Niva, M., 2009. Muuttuva syöminen – yksilön vastuu ja yhteiskunta. *Kuluttajatutkimuskeskuksen vuosikirja.* Helsinki: Kuluttajatutkimuskeskus, pp. 45–60.

Marketdata, 2014. Press release: weight loss market sheds some dollars in 2013: momentum shifts from diet products to diet services, says Marketdata. [online] Available at: http://www.marketdataenterprises.com/wp-content/uploads/2014/01/Diet-Market-2014-Status-Report.pdf [Accessed 5 April 2016].

Markula, P., 2008. Governing obese bodies in a control society. *Junctures: The Journal for Thematic Dialogue*, 11, pp. 53–66.

Marshall, T. H., 1950. *Citizenship and social class and other essays*. Cambridge: Cambridge University Press.

McKenzie, L., 2015. *Getting by: estates, class and culture in austerity Britain*. Bristol: Policy Press.

Miettinen, S., 2015. Kirurgi: lihavuusleikkausten määrä pitäisi tuplata. *YLE*, 5 May. [online] Available at: http://yle.fi/uutiset/kirurgi_lihavuusleikkausten_maara_pitaisi_tuplata/7972164 [Accessed 23 March 2016].

Mifflin, M., 1997. *Bodies of subversion: a secret history of women and tattoo*. New York: PowerHouse Books.

Millman, M., 1980. *Such a pretty face: being fat in America*. New York: W. W. Norton & Company.

Ministry of Social Affairs and Health website, n.d. Private social and health services. Available at: http://stm.fi/yksityiset-sotepalvelut?p_p_id=56_INSTANCE_7SjjYVd YeJHp&p_p_lifecycle=0&p_p_state=normal&p_p_mode=view&p_p_col_ id=column-2&p_p_col_count=3&_56_INSTANCE_7SjjYVdYeJHp_languageId=en_ US [Accessed 9 October 2015].

Mitchell, G. R., and McTigue, K., 2007. The US obesity epidemic: metaphor, method, or madness? *Social Epistemology*, 21 (4), pp. 391–423.

Mommo, P., 2015. Suomalaiset eivät halua käyttää verorahoja ylipainon torjuntaan. *YLE* website, 5 May. [online] Available at: http://yle.fi/uutiset/suomalaiset_eivat_halua_ kayttaa_verorahoja_ylipainon_torjuntaan/7971526 [Accessed 23 March 2016].

Mulvey, L., 1975. Visual pleasure and narrative cinema. *Screen*, 16 (3), pp. 6–18.

Murray, S., 2008. *The "fat" female body*. Basingstoke: Palgrave Macmillan.

National Institute for Health and Welfare (Terveyden ja hyvinvoinnin laitos; THL), 2008. *National action plan to reduce health inequalities 2008–2011*. Publications of the Ministry of Social Affairs and Health 25. [online] Available at: http://urn.fi/ URN:NBN:fi–fe201504224868 [Accessed 23 March 2016].

The National Institute for Health and Welfare (THL), 2009. *Läskillä lukutaitoa*, 29 December [online] Available at: http://www.thl.fi/fi_FI/web/fi/tiedote?id=21864 [Accessed 4 June 2013].

Noll, S. M. and Fredrickson, B. L., 1998. A meditational model linking self-objectification, body shame and disordered eating. *Psychology of Women Quarterly*, 22, pp. 623–636.

OECD, 2014. *Health at a glance: Europe 2014*, OECD Publishing. [online] Available at: http://dx.doi.org/10.1787/health_glance_eur-2014-en [Accessed 23 March 2016].

Oksala, J., 2013. Feminism and neoliberal governmentality. *Foucault Studies*, 16, pp. 32–53.

Oliver, E.J., 2006. *Fat politics: the real story behind America's obesity epidemic*. New York: Oxford University Press.

Orbach, S., 1998 [1977 and 1982]. *Fat is a feminist issue: the anti-diet guide for women* [1977] and *Fat is a feminist issue II* [1982]. London: Arrow Books.

Orjala, A. 2015. Sote-mallista ei vielä päätöstä – "Jumppa jatkuu", *YLE*, 20 May. [online] Available at: http://yle.fi/uutiset/sote-mallista_ei_viela_paatosta_jumppa_jatkuu/ 8005798 [Accessed 24 March 2016].

Owen, L., 2012. Living fat in a thin-centric world: effects of spatial discrimination on fat bodies and selves. *Feminism & Psychology*, 22 (3), pp. 290–306.

Palosuo, H., et al., 2009. *Health inequalities in Finland: trends in socioeconomic health differences 1980–2005*. Publications of the Ministry of Social Affairs and Health: 2009:9. [online] Available at: http://urn.fi/URN:NBN:fi-fe201504224334 [Accessed 23 March 2016].

Paloyo, A. R., Reichert, A. R., Reinermann, H., and Tauchmann, H., 2011. The causal link between financial incentives and weight loss: an evidence-based survey of the literature. *Ruhr Economic Papers* 290, Rheinisch-Westfälisches Institut für Wirtschaftsforschung (RWI), Essen.

Pausé, C., Wykes, J., and Murray S. eds., 2014. *Queering fat embodiment.* Farnham: Ashgate.

Peterson, A., and Lupton, D. 1996. *The new public health: discourses, knowledges, strategies.* London: Sage.

Puhl, R., and Brownell, K., 2001. Bias, discrimination, and obesity. *Obesity Research*, 9, pp. 778–805.

Puhl, R., and Brownell, K., 2003. Ways of coping with obesity stigma: review and conceptual analysis. *Eating Behaviours*, 4, pp. 53–78.

Rail, G., Holmes, D., and Murray, S., 2010. The politics of evidence on "domestic terrorists": obesity discourse and their effects. *Social Theory and Health*, 8 (3), pp. 259–279.

Rich, E., Harjunen, H., and Evans, J., 2006. Normal gone bad: exploring discourses of health and the female body in schools. In: Twohig, P., and Kalitzkus, V. eds. *Bordering biomedicine: making sense of health, illness and disease.* Amsterdam and New York: Rodopi Press, pp. 177–196.

Riihelä, M., Sullström, R., Suoniemi, I., and Tuomala, M., 2002. *Recent trends in income inequality in Finland.* Helsinki: Labour Institute for Economic Research.

Rinta-Tassi, M., 2015. Lihava on lihava omasta syystään, *YLE*, 5 May. [online] Available at: http://yle.fi/uutiset/kysely_lihava_on_lihava_omasta_syystaan/7973857 [Accessed 23 March 2016].

Rodan, D., Ellis, K., and Lebeck, P., 2014. *Disability, obesity and ageing: popular media identifications.* Farnham: Ashgate.

Romero-Corral, A., Montori, V. M., Somers, V. K., Korinek, J., Thomas, R. J., Allison, T. G., Mookadam, F., and Lopez-Jimenez, F., 2006. Association of bodyweight with total mortality and with cardiovascular events in coronary artery disease: A systematic review of cohort studies. *The Lancet*, 19, 368 (9536), pp. 666–78.

Rose, N., 1999. *Powers of freedom: reframing political thought.* Cambridge: The Cambridge University Press

Rothblum, E., and Solovay, S., 2009. *The fat studies reader.* New York: New York University Press.

Saguy, A., 2013. *What's wrong with fat?* New York: Oxford University Press.

Saguy, A., and Riley, K. W., 2005. Weighing both sides: morality, mortality, and framing contests over obesity. *Journal of Health Politics, Policy and Law*, 30 (5), pp. 869–921.

Sarlio-Lähteenkorva, S., 1999. *Losing weight for life?: social, behavioural and health-related factors in obesity and weight loss maintenance.* Department of Public Health, University of Helsinki.

Sarlio-Lähteenkorva, S., Silventoinen, K., and Lahelma, E., 2004. Relative weight and income at different levels of socioeconomic status. *American Journal of Public Health*, 94 (3), pp. 468–472.

Saukko, P., 1995. Tyttörukat kulttuurin ansassa: syömähäiriöt ja niiden esittämisen politiikka. *Tiedotustutkimus*, 2, pp. 40–54.

Schenk, T., 2015. Booked #3: what exactly is neoliberalism? *Dissent* Magazine, 2 April. [online] Available at: http://www.dissentmagazine.org/blog/booked-3-what-exactly-is-neoliberalism-wendy-brown-undoing-the-demos [Accessed 24 March 2016].

Schoenfielder, L., and Wieser. B. eds., 1989 [1983]. *Shadow on a tightrope: writings by women on fat oppression.* Iowa City, IA: Aunt Lute.

Sharma, A. M., and Kushner, R. F., 2009. A proposed clinical staging system for obesity. *International Journal of Obesity*, 33, pp. 289–295.

Sharp, L. A., 2000. The commodification of the body and its parts. *Annual Review of Anthropology*, 29, pp. 287–328.

Shilling, C., 1993. *The body and social theory*. London: Sage.

Singer, E., 2011. The measured life. *MIT Technology Review*, 21 June. [online] Available at: https://www.technologyreview.com/s/424390/the-measured-life/#/set/id/500361/ [Accessed 24 March 2016].

Sivonen, E., 2014. Lihavuus on riski puolustuskyvylle: reilu ylipaino on riski palve-lusturvallisuudelle. *Ruotuväki* [online] Available at: http://www.puolustusvoimat. fi/wcm/0a7451004329fdffa2ede2796152065b/Ruotuvaki%2B5_2014%2Blow. pdf%3FMOD%3DAJPERES [Accessed 12 December 2015].

Skeggs, B., 1997. *Formations of class and gender: becoming respectable*. London: Sage.

Skeggs, B., 2005. The making of class and gender through visualizing moral subject formation. *Sociology*, 39 (5), pp. 965–982.

Solovay, S., 2000. *Tipping the scales of justice: fighting weight-based discrimination*. Amherst, MA: Prometheus Books.

Solovay, S., and Rothblum, E., 2009. Introduction. In: Rothblum, E., and Solovay, S., eds. *The fat studies reader*. New York: New York University Press, pp. 1–2.

Sontag, S., 2002 [1978 and 1989]. *Illness as metaphor* and *Aids and its metaphors*. London: Penguin Books.

Squires, S., 1998. About your BMI: body mass index optimal weight threshold lowered. *The Washington Post*, Thursday, June 4. [online] Available at: http://www.washingtonpost. com/wp-srv/style/guideposts/fitness/optimal.htm [Accessed 24 March 2016].

Stunkard, A. J., and Sorensen, T. I. A., 1993. Obesity and socioeconomic status: a complex relation. *New England Journal of Medicine*, 32914, pp. 1036–1037.

Sutton, B., 2010. *Bodies in crisis: culture, violence and women's resistance in neoliberal Argentina*. New Brunswick, NJ: Rutgers University Press.

Tarkiainen, L., Martikainen, P., Laaksonen, M., and Valkonen, T., 2011. Trends in life expectancy by income from 1988 to 2007: decomposition by age and cause of death. *J Epidemiol Community Health*, 4 March [online] Available at: http://jech.bmj.com/ content/early/2011/03/04/jech.2010.123182.full.pdf [Accessed 11 April 2016].

The WHO Global Database on Body Mass Index, n.d. BMI classification. [online] Available at: http://apps.who.int/bmi/index.jsp?introPage=intro_3.html [Accessed 24 March 2016].

Thompson, K., 1998. *Moral panics*. Hove: Psychology Press.

Tovar, V., 2012. *Hot and heavy: fierce fat girls on life, love and fashion*. Berkeley, CA: Seal Press.

Turner, B., 1991 [1982]. The discourse of diet. In: Featherstone, M., Hepworth, M., and Turner, B. S., eds. *The body: social process and cultural theory*. London: Sage, pp. 157–169.

Valkendorff, T. 2014. Lihavuus "itse aiheutettuna ongelmana". Argumentteja Internetin keskustelupalstalta. *Sosiaalilääketieteellinen aikakauslehti*, 31, pp. 4–17.

Vaughn, W. B., Baruth, M., Beets, M. W., Durstine, L., Jihong, L., and Blair, S. N., 2014. Fitness vs. fatness on all-cause mortality: a meta-analysis. *Progress in Cardiovascular Diseases*, Special issue: Obesity and Obesity Paradox in Cardiovascular Diseases, 56 (4), pp. 382–390.

Ventura, P. 2012. *Neoliberal culture: living with American neoliberalism*. Farnham: Ashgate.

Wann, M., 2009, Foreword: fat studies: an invitation to revolution In: Rothblum, E. and Solovay, S., eds. *The fat studies reader*, pp. x–xi.

Wen, C. P, Cheng, D., Tsai SP, *et al.*, 2009. Are Asians at greater mortality risks for being overweight than Caucasians?: Redefining obesity for Asians". *Public Health Nutr.*, 12, pp. 497–506.

Wessel, T., Arant, C. S., Olson, M. B., Johnson, B. D., Reis, S. E. *et al.*, 2004. Relationship of physical fitness vs Body Mass Index with coronary artery disease and cardiovascular events in women. *Journal of the American Medical Association*, 292 (10), pp. 1179–1187.

Wingard, J., 2012. *Branded bodies, rhetoric, and the neoliberal nation-state*. Plymouth: Lexington Books.

Wolf, N., 1991 [1990]. *The beauty myth*. London: Vintage.

Working Group for the National Obesity Programme, 2013. Lihavuus laskuun – Hyvinvointia ravinnosta ja liikunnasta. [Overcoming obesity – wellbeing from healthy nutrition and physical activity]. National Obesity Programme 2012–2015. National Institute for Health and Welfare (THL). Directions 13/2013. pp. 58.

World Bank, 1993. *World development report: investing in health*. New York: Oxford University Press.

Wrede, S., Henriksson, L., Host, H., Johansson, S., and Dybbroe, B., 2008. *Care work in crisis: reclaiming the Nordic ethos of care*. Lund: Studentlitteratur.

Wright, J., and Harwood, V. eds., 2011. *Biopolitics and the "obesity epidemic": governing bodies*. London: Routledge.

Wykes, J., 2014. Introduction: why queering fat embodiment? In: Pausé, C., Wykes, J., and Murray, S., eds. *Queering fat embodiment*. Farnham: Ashgate, pp. 1–13.

YLE, 2010a. Katainen tekisi keskustan uudesta johtajasta myös pääministerin, *YLE*, 9 February. [online] Available at: http://yle.fi/uutiset/katainen_tekisi_keskustan_uudesta_johtajasta_myos_paaministerin/5506350 [Accessed 24 March 2016].

YLE, 2010b. Läskillä lukutaitoa-kampanja toi 1,4 miljoonaa Nepaliin, *YLE*, 14 June. [online] Available at: http://yle.fi/uutiset/laskilla_lukutaitoa_-kampanja_toi_14_miljoonaa_nepaliin/5580788 [Accessed 24 March 2016].

Yliaska, V., 2014. *Tehokkuuden toiveuni: uuden julkishallinnon historia Suomessa 1970-luvulta 1990-luvulle*. Helsinki: Into Kustannus.

Index